D1058577

Playing with Trumpets

A ROCK'N'ROLL APPRENTICESHIP

by **Micky Moody**

Playing with Trumpets

A ROCK'N'ROLL APPRENTICESHIP

by **Micky Moody**

First published in 2006
by SAF Publishing

SAF Publishing Ltd.
149 Wakeman Road, London.
NW10 5BH
ENGLAND

email: info@safpublishing.com
www.safpublishing.com

ISBN 10: 0 946719 86 1
ISBN 13: 978 0 946719 86 0

Printed in England by the Cromwell Press, Trowbridge, Wiltshire.

When I remember bygone days
I think how evening follows morn;
So many I loved were not yet dead,
So many I love were not yet born.

Ogden Nash

Acknowledgements

Thanks to all who have helped along the way, especially:

Dad, for being there when I needed that guitar..

Joe and Gladys Bradley for getting the Road Runners on the road.

John McCoy for helping me on my way.

Amanda for support and extreme patience.

Paul Newcombe, and Dave and Mick at SAF Publishing.

Contents

Monsters Of Rock,
Castle Donington,
August 1981

'On the instrument of the Devil—Micky Moody!'

The hyped-up voice that bellowed out of the gigantic public address system was greeted with the ecstatic cheers of 50,000 rock fans that hit me full on. Devil's instrument or not, my slide guitar solo spot had become an integral part of Whitesnake's classic hard-rock sound; a blues-tinged piece of individuality that inspired a communicative response from the audience. I hit a chord and stared ahead, my slide finger vibrating with intensity as I gradually swelled the instrument's volume control right up to number ten. Physical presence and powerful amplification created a state of sustained euphoria, as I held high a clenched fist to salute the faithful—an exultant gesture towards the hedonistic life-force we had become part of. The Seventies had a lot to answer for!

Yes, this was indeed another world, light years away from the college-cum-club circuit of entertaining that I'd grown used to prior to my involvement with David Coverdale. I had in fact, become a rock star, an icon of the denim-clad masses and in some people's estimation, a lucky bastard. Yet, I was troubled. Mismanagement, greed and far too many late nights had sown the seeds of mistrust and the roots were spreading. Within a matter of months, the travelling circus would reach the end of that long road and the good times would cross over into the land of legendary tales and rocklore. But where there's an ending, there's always a beginning. Here's mine.

Bargains and Brylcreem

'Dad, can I have a guitar?'

'What? These groups won't last forever you know, big bands'll be back. Learn the trumpet like Eddie Calvert.'

'But I want a guitar. I'll learn to play it, honest.'

'Well you'd better, I'm not wasting more money.'

My father was a very practical man whose way of thinking implied that anything bought must prove to be value for money. The idea of another instrument standing idly in the corner like "that bloody piano", may have brought back memories of his tough childhood during the Twenties,

However, "that bloody piano", probably purchased for next to nothing from one of his cronies at the pub, was intended to bring a bit of culture into the household, courtesy of my sister Eileen.

She was soon nominated, unknowingly, to take piano lessons, though the idea never materialised. Consequently, the piano stood silent, apart from my father's occasional doodlings, when, after tea, he would roll up his shirtsleeves and attempt to persuade the dissipated keyboard to lull the rest of us into some sort of musical nirvana by striking the white notes with his right index finger.

He always failed.

His original idea was to impress us all by playing the melody line from the classic song 'Blue Skies'. This was quickly brought to a halt, due mainly to a complete lack of musical education, no technique whatsoever, and partial blindness brought about by cigarette smoke billowing up from the Woodbine pursed between his lips. What transpired was a sound not dissimilar to lemmings diving head first from the top of a piano onto its keyboard. Only my mother could supersede these tonally-challenged purges when she cleaned the keys once a week with a duster. In fact, the melodies she accidentally delivered were often more tuneful.

The Moodys seemed destined for musical obscurity, though my Aunt Gertie had developed a piano style that offered an interesting blend of Winifred Atwell and Les Dawson, and my uncle Bernie could make dogs howl when he vamped on a harmonica. Fortunately for the world at large, both of them reserved their particular talents for family get-togethers, wedding party nights, and New Year's Eve celebrations. Professional and even semi-professional musicians were an unknown commodity in our lineage.

My particular patronym is of old English origin, best described as of a category of surnames derived from a physical or personal characteristic of the original bearer. A definite case of 'by name—by nature'. The family tree, or in my case twig, seemed to bear few roots beyond those of my grandfather, though his limited knowledge proved rather interesting. His father was a cockney sea captain who spent more time in the port of Middlesbrough than the port of London, thus making a relocation inevitable. Bow Bells blood or not, the Moodys soon became acclimatised to the chilly North East.

On my mother's side, a similar family twig existed. Unlike the Moodys of Middlesbrough, she hailed from the next stop down the line— Thornaby, the last bastion of North Yorkshire. Staying on the train you soon cross the River Tees and enter County Durham, a stretch of land leading eventually to an inevitable change of accent.

My inherited birthright of growing up in the north east of England— the special privilege bestowed upon its sons and daughters is the right to eat, drink and sleep football. Children were therefore tucked into bed on cold winter's nights and lulled to sleep, listening to folklore, where great gods with names like Mannion, Hardwick and Clough defeated armies of southern warriors wearing baggy shorts, protected only with shin pads and Brylcreem. The battleground on which these greasy confrontations took place was known as Ayresome Park, in the kingdom of Central Middlesbrough. It was to this hallowed shrine that my uncle John took me one crisp Saturday afternoon in the autumn of 1957. Now, it's customary for fathers to escort their offspring to such gatherings, but mine was probably at the Workingman's Institute, bartering over some Czechoslovakian vacuum cleaner or a Second World War tent, cloth cap rakishly angled and half-hidden by the smoke from his Woodbine.

To be fair, my dad was there for many fixtures, relating first-hand accounts of the great performances he'd witnessed.

'Oh aye, son, I remember seeing Stanley Mortenson score with the back of 'is 'ead from the 'alf-way line,' he reminisced.

I imagined the reaction from his team-mates. Brief handshakes and a trot back to the centre-circle, no doubt. Hugs and kisses were strictly for the over-paid prima donnas of the future.

If Uncle John was at the same match, he was either too shy or too modest to mention it. He was a kindly soul who looked like a cross between Uncle Fester from the Addams family and a steward from the Jarrow hunger march. Malingering seemed to be his greatest asset; in fact, his inert nature sometimes gave you the impression that he'd been anaesthetised. Reasons for his failure to be accepted by His Majesty's Armed Forces during the Second World War were never discussed, though I suspect he preferred to stay at home with his mother, my nana. However, his enlistment to the Home Guard was essential, and judging by photographic evidence, he wore his uniform with pride.

'That Anthony Eden,' he recalled, 'he wanted to call us the Local Volunteers Defence, but Churchill said, "No, it's got to be the Home Guard".'

Years later he gave me his khaki cap, and I wore it with relish as a Penny Arrow Bar and an orange squash were placed into my gloved hands, and we climbed the Bovril-stained steps to witness the great encounter.

Memories of that impressionable day paint an image of a vast space, and a pitch that shone like a fairy dell snooker table without the pockets. It looked beautiful; so smooth and so green. We made our way to the area behind one of the goals, a move easily negotiated, as the crowd for this reserve match numbered no more than a thousand. It was rather a small gathering in a stadium capable of holding around forty times that many. I struggled with my toffee bar, innocently oblivious of such things as dental cavities, drills and dentists with halitosis. Suddenly, a musical fanfare rang out through some rather tinny tannoys, heralding the appearance of the players, who trotted proudly from their dressing room tunnel. I assumed it was a tunnel. Maybe it was a door and they just entered from the street. They did look fit though, albeit rather oily. The rest of the afternoon has receded into the mists of time, but I was converted to a game whose pleasures I would pursue for many years to come. The same dedication would later be applied to my chosen instrument, the guitar. In the meantime, there was a childhood to get on with.

Our very first television set was a black and white 14-inch model made by a company called Murphy. All I can say is that *Watch With Mother* was a big influence—and Richard Greene was Robin Hood. How did he stay so clean amidst all that blood and muck?

Football matches were few and far between, and for teams who played in black and white, like Bolton Wanderers, Derby County, Tottenham Hotspurs and Fulham, commentary was not only sociable, it was essential. I have distant memories of the 1957 FA Cup Final, when Aston Villa beat Manchester United by two goals to one, denying United the 'double'. Matt Busby's 'babes' were everyone's favourites, destined for European domination until disaster struck at Munich airport the following February. Seven of the United squad perished and the whole country went into mourning. At school the following day, some of the teachers (and pupils) were visibly moved as we offered up prayers in their memory. I can't imagine what it must have been like in Manchester. Thirteen days later, Billy Foulkes and Harry Gregg, two of the survivors, led the team out against Sheffield Wednesday. They were true heroes.

The chart-topping backdrop to 1958 was monopolised by solo singers. Elvis, Jerry Lee Lewis, Perry Como and even someone called Marvin Rainwater all had number ones alongside Connie Francis and Tommy Edwards (who?). My father's aforementioned piano assassinations now included Michael Holliday's 'The Story of My Life'. The story of dad's life was that of a man who should never have been allowed near a piano. His approach had all the finesse of a disturbed demolition worker. He didn't so much play the notes as poke them into submission. Maybe it was a case of being in the wrong place at the wrong time, as avant-garde jazz clubs had yet to appear in Middlesbrough—the equivalent of Cecil Taylor turning up at the Welders and Sheet Metalworkers Club.

Ignoring rockers, pop singers, and anything else of a lively nature, my mother went out and bought 'I'll Walk With God' by Mario Lanza, which was probably my first experience of a musical dirge. My reaction was comparable to being offered a council flat on the outskirts of Gdansk.

Due to lack of interest, the piano was wheeled off to the scrap heap. A trendy bureau immediately occupied its position against the living room wall and housed the family's limited book collection. Neither of my parents took any particular interest in literature, though my mother would read the odd publication on religious matters.

On Christmas Day, Santa Claus was kind enough to deposit a copy of *The Big Book of Football Champions* into my pillowcase of presents. The front cover showed an action shot of a young Bobby Charlton, sporting a head of hair so lush, that even Ken Dodd would have been proud to call it his own. What happened Bobby, did you wash it in sulphuric acid or something? By 1962, he'd be combing it with a trowel. The back cover displayed a shot of two Scotsmen, namely Younger and Haddock, trying in vain to prevent England's first goal in their 4-0 defeat at Hampden Park. Oh, hard luck, lads! Cast between these impressive bindings was a world of heroes and icons whose actions I came to regard with the utmost respect, though they all seemed to look older than they actually were. No nancy-boys in them days; and they probably earned next to nothing. Nicolas Anelka wouldn't have stood a chance.

Some people think that football is a matter of life and death...
I can assure them it is much more serious than that. – Bill Shankley.

As my passion for the game grew, every possible moment was spent kicking something around, and as the family did not possess a cat, I learned how to improvise with rubber balls, balloons, rolled up socks or beanbags. Even apples and oranges suffered at the hands of my feet. Well, I didn't really have hands on my feet, but you know what I mean. The obsession was not limited to indoors either. Street signs, gateways and brick walls, would regularly come under fire from my industrious feet.

'He's out there again,' remarked one of the neighbours.

'I think 'es football mad. Too many Iron Jelloids,' offered another.

I didn't care; it was a lot more fun than long-distance running, though my fitness and general health was often hindered by continuous sore throats. After one too many bouts of tonsillitis, my parents decided it was time to take Dr Blenkinsop's advice and have the offending tissue removed. It proved a traumatic experience, administered by insensitive people who, for many years, left me with an acute fear of hospitals and their employees. When I regained consciousness, a fat nurse appeared at my side.

'Ah, you're awake.'

'Visiting time is in two hours, would you like to eat some scrambled eggs?'

'No,' I croaked, aware that my recent tonsillectomy would not allow such activity. She smiled, before continuing with her bedpan duties.

Somewhere in Chicago, a down-hearted blues singer was better off than me. At least he was capable of howling for his baby.

Visiting hours brought a steady stream of gift-laden relatives and friends, all eager to present bottles of Lucozade and comics to convalescing loved ones. Though my croak had improved, forgiveness towards the violators would be a long time coming, and my own visitors received little in the way of reciprocal chat. My dad tried to cheer me up by extolling the talents of the Three Monarchs, a trio of humorous harmonica players that featured a buffoon with a nanny-goat beard called Cedric.

By dusk I was alone and still wallowing in misery when suddenly, from somewhere in the distance, I heard the voices of mischievous children chanting in unison:

Whirly whirly custard, snot and bogie pie
All mixed up with a dead dog's eye
Cold blooded sandwich's spread on thick
And all washed down with a bucket full of sick

My lack of appetite remained for some time.

Due to my age and general constitution, recovery from my tonsillectomy was swift and trouble-free. I was in good shape physically, but a sensitive side was beginning to show. My mother put this down to 'nerves', a curiously common condition in post-war, peaceful, optimistic Britain. I'd put it down to a developing creative streak and an unpleasant experience in the operating theatre at the Royal Infirmary Hospital, Middlesbrough.

As a reward for being a brave my parents took me to see Mother Shipton's wishing well, a tourist attraction in north Yorkshire. My dad explained to me that the well had magical properties and that if you tossed a coin into it and made a silent wish, it would eventually come true. He then suggested that I wish for a golden trumpet like the one supposedly played by 'Mr Trumpet himself', Eddie Calvert. Why, so he could play it? Jesus, we'd already suffered his piano playing; imagine what aural damage a tone-deaf steel-erector could do with something like that in his hands. And anyway, if it had been solid gold, I'd have been unable to lift it, let alone play the bloody thing!

Charles Buchan's *Football Monthly* was eagerly awaited, and I began to build up quite a collection of annuals and match programmes. They were avidly studied until my knowledge of the game began to impress my elders. Sunday afternoons dissolved into football trivia quizzes featuring yours truly and yes, you've guessed it, the head of the household avec cronies, fresh in from the lunch time session at the pub. An innocent method of exploitive behaviour guaranteed that I could receive sixpence for every correct answer, until the intoxicated jury took their respite with tea and cigarettes. Pretty soon I'd saved up enough money to pay for the prehistoric football boots that the lads in the saloon bar had persuaded my father to consider for me. When he mentioned the possibility of this little 'bargain' to me, I remonstrated that these hideous creations had last been employed during a game between Woolwich Arsenal and Old Corinthians. I was having none of it, and would wait until Christmas for a more up-to-date pair, preferably in continental-style black, and hopefully without leather studs, high ankles and laces made from hemp.

These wishes eventually materialised. I was finally granted the boots of my dreams in a Yuletide package that also included a copy of *The Topical Times Football Book, edition No.1*. Guess whose image graced the front cover? Yes, Bobby Charlton, still in possession of most of his hair. This time the back cover showed only a single Scotsman—a goalkeeper named Jimmy Brown of Kilmarnock. The inside of the dust cover promised:

A host of memorable pictures. Giants of the game in full colour. Thrilling moments from big matches in vivid action. Big-size team groups from the honours list, plus star articles by star players and—the Bobby Charlton story.

At last, we could read about the meteoric rise of a man who was born without hair, grew it, then lost it again. Whilst doing so, he became a footballing genius, survived the Munich air crash, then appeared on *Double Your Money*, where he won a thousand pounds by answering questions on pop music. To celebrate his achievements he decided to ignore the dolly birds, nightclubs and low-life agents and buy a new car instead. Wise man. Over the years, and especially during my time with Whitesnake, I met quite a few name players, most of them music fans, who were genuine hard working, modest men. I'm not sure I could say the same nowadays.

I began to take an interest in pop music via the family portable radio, though I think my senses had first been activated one Saturday afternoon in Woolworths' record department when I heard 'Red River Rock' by Johnny and the Hurricanes. I found their raw brand of rocking instrumentals very appealing. The Light Programme was the main source of popular music, giving way in the evenings to Radio Luxembourg. To augment this massive choice I also had access to Eileen's recently acquired Cliff Richard and the Shadows records (the soundtrack to *Snow White and the Seven Dwarves* having become distinctly passé). I loved the Shadows, and would soon become one of the legions of impersonators miming along to 'Apache', in my case substituting Hank Marvin's trademark Fender Stratocaster with a cricket bat. Some of these aspiring guitar heroes were lucky enough to have older brothers who'd bought the latest stateside recordings by Elvis Presley, Little Richard, Jerry Lee Lewis and a host of first generation rockers. We had to make do with records by Cliff and the Shads, Lonnie Donegan and 'Little Donkey' by the Beverley Sisters, so sod 'em.

Football Feaver

A place on the school football team was usually reserved for the fourth or final year students, though the odd 'third-yearer' could suitably impress the sports master enough to break rank. And so, a small yet impressionable nine year old, familiar with elementary soccer techniques and questionable taste in pop music, found himself on an equal footing (so to speak) with the older lads. I played in goal, wearing the school team jumper, a navy blue affair with a polo-neck that covered most of my face. The arms were so long, if I'd cut off the excess material, there would have been enough to make a pair of tights for a giraffe.

We lost by 2 goals to 1, a reasonable result considering that the opponent's centre forward, the formidable Don Harker, was only an inch or two shorter than the Colossus of Rhodes. I knew my cards were marked when, prior to the kick-off, he offered me a piece of chewing gum. A cigarette and a blindfold might have been more appropriate. He scored both his teams goals, the second from the penalty spot. He administered the kick with such force, that it bent my hand back to form a right angle with my arm, a position it held for the rest of the day. When I waved goodbye, it gave the impression that I was showing off an invisible tray of drinks.

Sundays in the Moody household would have been an eye-opener for any visiting gourmet. For lunch, the Yorkshire pudding would be served as a starter, whilst mint sauce was always regarded as the perfect complement to roast beef. Afterwards we would settle down and enjoy a film on TV or listen to the synchronised snoring courtesy of my dad and Uncle Bernie. It didn't get any better at tea-time either, when we were encouraged to eat plenty of brown bread and butter with tinned fruit and condensed milk. It filled us up. My mother showed Bernie a letter from the government.

'Look, they've finished with conscription. Michael won't have to go into the army now.' 'That's a pity,' replied Bernie. 'It made a man out of me.'

I got the impression that she was not entirely convinced.

The rules of soccer are basically simple—if it moves, kick it; if it doesn't move, kick it until it does—Phil Woosnam.

The following term I became a regular in the team, eagerly awaiting mid-afternoon on a Friday, when the list of budding ball-bashers would be pinned up for all to see:

St. Alphonsus Junior School vs Victoria Road Junior School

Would these boys please report to Mr Drury at playtime:
McPartland, Marshall, O'Grady, Durie, Taylor, Brotheston, Dixon, Moody,
McIlvaney, Gallagher, Connelly

We would dutifully pick up our playing kit, half-listen to a brief pep talk, then bound back into the playground as pleased as punch, football strips rolled up and clutched tightly to deter jealous fingers. We definitely had one up on the rest of the lads, some of who glared at us with envy and reluctant respect. One or two of the girls smiled at me; I was developing an ego! The following day we stuffed Victoria Road by 3 goals to 0 and I scored a beauty.

'Hello girls.'

'Oh, hello handsome football hero, we just love your short grey trousers and string vest!' Oh well—dream on.

Playing football in the school playground was a risky business. Lookouts posted at vantage points would employ precursory vocal sounds to warn us of approaching teachers. We usually managed to avoid capture by slipping the ball into the hood of an innocent passer-by's duffel coat, which then allowed us to slip our hands into our pockets and sometimes we'd nonchalantly whistle 'Dixie'. If caught, we'd be made to atone for our sins with a humbling visit to the headmistress, Sister Mary Vincent, a nun with all the charm of a Siberian prison guard. Corporal punishment was usually administered with a bamboo cane, though the employment of a chair leg sometimes helped soothe away her tight-lipped frustrations. Ironically, her particular order was called the Sisters of Mercy.

Back on the football pitch, I persevered with my attacking style a la Jimmy Greaves—a long kick to the winger, a dash towards the penalty area and hopefully, a return pass. If a return pass came my way I'd have a go, though reciprocation was never assured. My most memorable effort occurred in a game against Marton Road Juniors, when I half-volleyed a shot into the left-hand corner of the netless goal. My dad was standing behind the posts and my effort almost sliced his cap off. Irrespective of the fact that I didn't like being tackled, having to play in the rain or heading the ball, my attraction to the game was complete. Alas, a few weeks later, my ego trip diminished somewhat, when I was dropped in favour of a replacement, who was a friend and neighbour. Life's a bitch.

In search of some *Boy's Own*-type of adventure, I decided to join the St Alphonsus Boy Scouts, and after no time, was well on the way to gaining my 'tenderfoot' badge. This preliminary merit could be acquired by possessing a uniform to stitch it to, and by having the ability to tie a selection of knots, such as the reef, the clove-hitch or the granny. These were, apparently, universally-proven techniques that would stand me in good stead for the future, though I've managed to get by so far on shoe laces alone. The Boy Scouts' motto was "Be prepared", though the reason for adopting such a vigilant stance was never fully explained until a friend from a rival pack confided in me.

'I'm going to join your scout group,' he informed me somewhat seriously.

'Why?' I pressed.

'Because our pack leader keeps feeling my arse!'

I failed my 11-Plus examination, which was not totally unexpected, and though the result was a disappointment, I had no particular peer pressure to maintain. Considering that I was only ten at the time (my 11th birthday was during the summer holidays), I shouldn't have been sitting the bloody thing anyway. According to the local education committee, I'd done well enough to be awarded 'selective status', whatever that meant. However, there was both A and O levels to work towards, plus the City and Guilds which, to me, were really diplomas of merit for blokes with spanners. However, parents of northern working-class lads were happy to see their offspring 'get a proper job'; e.g. motor mechanic; plumber; electrician; horseracing expert etc, and as work was plentiful in those days, I suffered no remorse at my failure. Anyway, I'd probably be an apprentice at Middlesbrough F.C. before too long, so why worry about daft things like exam results. Goodbye junior school—hello secondary modern.

Got Wimples On Me Head

Dear St Thomas, cherished patron
With thy help be ever near
May our 'credo', strong and certain
With one voice ring loud and clear

St Thomas's was more than just secondary modern; it was extremely modern. Having opened only a year or two before my introduction, it boasted a state-of-the-art gymnasium, science lab, art class, music room, cookery class and both metalwork and woodwork shops. There was a full sized assembly hall with curtained stage, not to mention playing fields, bicycle sheds and life-threatening asbestos ceilings. Due to my 'selective status' I was placed in the 'technical stream', that is, amongst individuals with a bit more potential than some of the others, though structured in such a way that shirkers could be relegated to 'dumbo' level at the end of term. I vowed to avoid the pachyderm plane at all costs and to my credit, managed to stay within the acceptable stage throughout the duration, though the phrase 'must try harder' would become a tedious associate.

Prior to my initiation into senior school, my parents had been required to fork out a small fortune for my school uniform, an uninspired black and grey creation with just a hint of pink in the tie. A blazer with zoot-suit shoulders and orang-utan arms was draped over my skinny frame while I listened to my mother's voice uttering that dreaded expedient, 'You'll grow into it'. Sure, I'd grow into it. All that was required was a crash course in bodybuilding and a few days of agonising arm stretching on a rack. The cap was decidedly un-hip and spent most of its time folded up in my pocket. I was not alone in this practice.

Once familiar with my new surroundings, it seemed a good idea to set about establishing myself where it really mattered—on the football pitch. The preceding three or four years of daily kick-abouts and Saturday morning junior school games had proven to be beneficial, and the sports master complimented me on my "intelligent use of the ball". I was to become automatic choice for the preliminary side, a motley crew of classmates and playground cronies of various heights and girths. Unfortunately, I was unable to administer the equivalent "intelligent use of" during the maths class and came to dread the Monday morning showdown with the fearsome Mr Kelly. Mathematics was not my forte, as he often reminded me. Though brusque in many ways, he was capable of mild compassion. Spotting my *Classics Illustrated* comic of James Fenimore Cooper's *The Last of the Mohicans*, he raised his eyes slightly.

'Ah, the last of the mucky 'un's! What do you think of Cooper's work then, Moody?' he asked.

'He writes good comics, sir,' I replied honestly.

He regarded me with a mixture of contempt and sadness—that look of wounded academia. We never discussed literature again. Furthermore, he suggested I turn to Saint Jude for help. Spurred on by a sense of curiosity, I made further inquiries and discovered that the aforementioned was the patron saint of lost causes. Was he trying to tell me something?

An interest in history, geography and French gave way to bouts of nausea during physics, whilst managing to stay awake throughout the technical drawing class became difficult. My English has definitely improved with age and in the art class, a group of us once made a passable pterodactyl out of papier-mâché. The art teacher, Mr Kominsky, was, well, arty I suppose, and kept a flick knife in his desk drawer. Cool! He also liked music and would eventually play a small part in my early musical development.

Like most kids, I enjoyed 'the telly', especially Gerry and Sylvia Anderson's puppet series. Their first creation was a Wild West adventure with a magical twist called *Four Feather Falls* and starred Tex Tucker, a sheriff with ludicrously large eyebrows. The follow-up, *Supercar*, once again featured our little wooden hero with the accentuated brow, this time masquerading as Mike Mercury—super pilot. According to the theme tune, "It travels on land and under the sea and it can journey anywhere".

And it did—every week.

Advertising, though still in its infancy, was reaching a larger and, most importantly, captive audience. TV ads all seemed to be in black and white, though that may have had something to do with the fact that we only had a black and white television. Drip-dry shirts were the new craze, and Rael Brook celebrated their line with animated shirts frolicking to a catchy tune. Instantly memorable melodies also included "Green Line Mints with the soft chewy centres", and "Murray mints, Murray mints, too good to hurry mints", the latter being somewhat *Monty Python*-esque in its delivery. The downside to my television enjoyment was administered by my father, usually at newstime

'See, look at that,' he'd start, looking in my direction. 'You don't know you're born. Food on the table, clothes.' The accompanying images were of starving children in the Congo.

I've travelled far, the land and the sea
Beautiful places I've happened to be
One little town I'll never forget
Is Lourdes, the village of St Bernadette

My first taste of continental travel was arranged by my mother. As an active member of the Catholic Women's League, she'd decided to include Eileen and myself in the annual pilgrimage to Lourdes, that centre of faith, hope and merchandising. Dressed for fine weather and armed with stories of imminent miracles, the holy of the parish gathered at Middlesbrough railway station amid an air of motivated responsibility. There were some lesser endowed amongst us, including a thalidomide toddler and a number of handicapped. These poor souls were uppermost in people's minds and prayers; fingers were crossed for the big miracle. The initial stage of the journey, a train ride to somewhere on the south coast, was undertaken with the naive air of true amateur crusaders. Thankfully, we didn't have to suffer the onslaught of deranged Moors, though bouts of seasickness on the ferry contributed towards a miserable atmosphere during the remaining long hours of our penance. When we finally disembarked in the land of the baguette, somewhat green around the gills, we boarded a train so archaic, that its class structure started at third and ended at eighth. Our party was interned at seventh, granting the lucky ones a hardwood seating arrangement of arse-numbing proportions. The following twelve hours or so were indeed a test of faith.

Much of the initial camaraderie—based upon humility, good intentions and genuine belief—was soon dispelled during those remaining steam-driven miles. Petty arguments broke out due to tiredness and discomfort, though light relief was provided by daft-sounding place names, some of which I would grow to know and drink. Calvados, Cognac, Bordeaux and Armagnac all passed within a short bouquet of our carriage. I was, of course, far too young to appreciate this, though I've made up for it since. All that was missing was *Jacques D'Aniels*.

Having completed a journey that equated to almost the entire length of both England and France, we arrived at Lourdes looking like extras from a Boris Karloff film. Hotel. Bed. Sleep.

I awoke to the sound of familiar voices outside of the door.

'I'll get the kids up, then we'll eat. I'm flippin' starvin.'

My roommate, a boy with heavily callipered legs, echoed my mother's feelings.

'Cor, my stomach's rumbling,' he observed, reaching for his metal staff.

His matter-of-factness towards such an acute disability helped me to overcome my own awkwardness.

'D'ya think they serve Ready Brek, John?' I asked in all seriousness.

'Not in France. Probably Scott's Porridge Oats,' he answered accordingly.

'Ee, the bathrooms 'ave got footbaths in them.' I said.

The en-suite bathroom did indeed offer a small unusual-shaped receptacle, featuring hot and cold running water, and was of a size compatible to the average foot. After a nominal ablution I gave it a try. Its most unusual feature was the low-lying water dispenser that, I presumed, was intended to massage the underside of the foot during the wash. It was a number of years until I was shown the intended purpose of a bidet.

Regardless of the pervasive humility, the pleasant weather and surrounding views of the Pyrenees helped create a relaxed atmosphere. I came to the conclusion that we were on a sort of holiday with a conscience. At dinner time we were presented with sugar cubes, an unheard of commodity in the Moody household. With a little help from my roommate John, I smuggled a couple of handfuls back to the room, to keep as a special reserve in case of late night hunger attacks. We soon devised a game that would require a further supply when 'Hit the nun's nut' became our first excursion into naughtiness. We were joined by another lad and celebrated our independence with carefully aimed shots from our second floor eyrie, and onto the passing chaste craniums. Whilst the majority reacted in a startled manner, some showed no response whatsoever. We concluded that certain orders employed extra thick wimples in order to fend off the airborne projectiles. Our little bit of fun was terminated within the hour when one of our group spotted the goings-on from across the street and informed our mothers. Game over.

The next day we experienced the real thing. A walk to the revered grotto of the visitation required us to pass shops dealing in mementos and obligatory candles. The latter would feature heavily in the nightly processions, an emotional sight I was yet to encounter. A round-faced shopkeeper with bushy eyebrows gazed dolefully in our direction, like a depressed owl, while my feelings were roused by the sight of lesser mortals; the sick, the immobile and worst of all, the mentally retarded. Chucking sugar cubes at nuns paled into insignificance—this was the real world. Sadly, the real world reared its commercial head on the return journey, where the souvenir shops caught us with our humble bits exposed. The small group of unrehearsed pilgrims, blessed by umpteen men of the cloth, wished to honour this special day with a token of remembrance. So, retracing our steps, we entered one of many shops only too willing to satisfy our needs.

The Ave Maria Gift Shop was one of many dealing in the kind of 'memorabilia' designed to encourage the recently motivated soul into parting with some of its recently acquired francs. Cynical but accurate. Let's face it, nobody was forced into a purchase, but an emotive response was appreciated by the shopkeepers. My mother was taken by a plastic music box effigy of St. Bernadette praying at the grotto. By turning the key a few times, a rendition of 'Ave Maria' was heard. What else? 'Rock with the Caveman' by Tommy Steele? I think not. In retrospect, the word 'experience' still resounds strongly.

The acute discomfort of the return journey was diminished only by our experiences a fortnight earlier. This time we were prepared for a shitty journey, though the more serious believers once again relished the opportunity to repent. What exactly did they do wrong?

We stopped at a station to stretch our legs, backs and imaginations when I spotted a pair of rural buskers. One played an accordion whilst the other accompanied him on acoustic guitar. My eyes soon focused on the guitarist, and though his efforts were elementary, he was worthy of my attention till we all climbed begrudgingly back on to the train.

My thoughts turned to buying comics once we were back home, especially *The Victor*, which featured a true schoolboy hero called Alf Tupper—the tough of the track. Alf was questionably the greatest athlete in the world, but his unorthodox lifestyle, which included a staple diet of fish and chips and a bus shelter for a home, caused not only headaches but also migraines for the Track Select Committee. He was traced only at the eleventh hour, and came bursting onto the track in a pair of baggy old shorts to win the Olympic gold medal in record time. Not a man to seek attention, he would shun the awards ceremony and donate his gong to a needy orphanage in an act of true inspiration to the poor underdog. He made Bob Geldof look like a Californian lawyer.

Comics could be educational too. I learned that the Red Indian, sorry, Native American word for ouch was Aaaaiiih!, because that was the word that appeared in their mouth-bubble when they got shot (as they always seemed to).

By the end of 1961, I'd settled in at school, made some new friends, and had amassed a small collection of singles including 'Cathy's Clown' by the Everley Brothers, 'F.B.I.' and 'The Frightened City' by the Shadows. That Christmas, my parents treated Eileen and myself on a trip to see Cliff Richard and the Shadows in pantomime at the Hippodrome Theatre in Stockton. The Shadows were starring both as the Shads and as occasional period-clad mischief-makers, and closed the show with a medley of their hits including 'Apache' and 'Man of Mystery'. It was my first live concert and I was deeply impressed. Back home I reached once more for my cricket bat and headed for the mirror, conscious of some early soul stirring and a desire to get my hands on a real guitar.

The following twelve months were not vintage ones for pop music, especially from a British perspective. Record companies in the States managed to produce quality numbers such as 'I Can't Stop Loving You' by Ray Charles, 'Hey Baby' by Bruce Channel and 'Good Luck Charm' by Elvis Presley. The best we could muster on this side of the pond was 'I Remember You' by Frank Ifield and 'Telstar' by the Tornados, which was also a chart topper in the US. Mind you, so was 'Stranger on the Shore' by Acker Bilk, but the less said about that the better. I liked instrumentals, notably ones that featured guitars (as opposed to bloody clarinets), and Johnny and the Hurricanes were a particular favourite. Meanwhile, my desire for a fretted friend remained unchallenged. Yes, 1962 was, to my recollection, a pretty non-eventful year for me, apart from my selection for the school preliminary football team, and a fortnight's stay at a former army camp near Hexham, known as Dukeswood Camp.

A great sense of excitement filled the coach as it headed north into the great unknown territories of Northumberland. Our summer break, organised by education authorities in Northumberland, Durham and North Yorkshire, was an early attempt at juvenile bonding. It was a simple exercise, devoid of Walkmans, Gameboys, mobile phones and videos, though we were allowed to listen to Radio Luxembourg for a while before lights out. Billeted in large wooden huts, we slept in bunk beds that, I soon learned, are fine providing the person above you is flatulently retentive. Lying in my bed on the first night, I experienced a depressing bout of homesickness, and I'm pretty sure I wasn't the only one. We ate in a canteen where every single sitting was accompanied by jars of jam. As it turned out, my jam-propelled fortnight at Dukeswood was a memorable affair, shared with old and new friends alike.

The camp housed a small cinema into which we trooped to watch *Calamity Jane*, staring that most quintessential of women, Doris Day, at her tomboy best, belting out 'The Deadwood Stage', 'The Black Hills of Dakota', 'Windy City' and 'Secret Love'. I'm convinced that if God had been depicted as a woman, she would have been cast in the image of our Doris. Now what do we have? The Anti-Doris in the shape of Pamela Anderson.

On the final night of our stay, the teachers organised a small concert featuring some pop music enthusiasts attempts to emulate their hero's hits to a piano accompaniment. For some reason or other, I was saddled with the task of performing Kenny Lynch's version of 'Up on the Roof', a tune not unfamiliar to me, though not a particular favourite. Standing self-consciously on the small stage, I executed a version that allowed both flat and sharp notes to mingle freely amongst a throng of gigglers and lip-biters. My cheeks grew redder by the verse. The prompted applause gave me more cause for embarrassment, until my head looked like a giant tomato with hair. I was glad to return to my seat and make way for the next sucker.

The early Sixties produced an interesting number of novelty records which, without doubt, enhanced the career of Charlie Drake, a vertically-challenged comedian who threw himself around with such unmitigated enthusiasm that he once rendered himself unconscious on live television. A feat that even Johnny Rotten failed to emulate. Drake could well have been the instigator of a new-wave of mirth-making by releasing a song entitled 'My Boomerang Won't Come Back' in 1961. However, the following year was vintage in the annals of daft songs. Starting with the short-arsed one's follow up, 'I Bent My Assagai', we were treated to 'What A Crazy World We're Living In', by Joe Brown, and a trio of gems from another comic actor, Bernard Cribbins. 'Hole In the Ground', 'Right Said Fred', and 'Gossip Calypso' left such an impression on my juvenile mind that I can still remember all the lyrics to 'Gossip Calypso' and the majority from the other two. Oh, and I know the words to Joe Brown's 'Crazy World' too! "Dad's gone down the dog track, mother's playing bingo……".

Sorry, I'll move on.

Before the year was out I'd made my own attempt at written humour in the form of a school essay featuring a character called Barnacube McSwine, an obvious simpleton, who worked on a toenail-cutting farm! It seemed that this particular form of chiropody caused such dissatisfaction amongst his customers, that the poor man, afraid for his life, or just a life, took flight. His journey of enlightenment took him to the town of Rhubarbsville, where he entered into pugilistic combat with a cock-eyed cat prior to returning home for a life of anonymity. The form teacher regarded my effort with a certain amount of wariness. I can't think why.

His recommendation that I should study the works of Dickens and Goethe was met with a blank response. Who the hell was "Gowth" when he was at home?

'Goerteh, boy, it is pronounced Goerteh.'

At Christmas, the teaching staff organised a nativity play, and I must have taken part in some sort of audition, and I was cast as one of the Three Wise Men and was lumbered with the immortal line:

'We have seen his star in the East, and have come to worship him.'

Unfortunately, my thick Middlesbrough accent translated this as:

'We 'ave seen 'is star in the east, and we 'ave cum to wership 'im.'

The teacher in charge was not impressed and insisted I stay behind "to develop my vowels." This little exercise was based entirely on the pronunciation of the words purple and work, and was, apparently, peculiar to young lads of northern origin. I walked home from school chanting like some obsessed Buddhist; 'wworrkk, ppurrpplle, wworrkk, ppurrpplle.' Come the big night I coasted through my line then, with almost a swagger, bowed before the newborn child to offer up my frankincense. Unfortunately, my wooden sword somehow became entangled in the back of my apparel, granting the audience a first-hand insight into the mysteries of biblical underwear.

Wise Men apparently wore football shorts.

1963. Ah, that's much better! The Beatles, the Rolling Stones, Mersey Beat in general, Jet Harris and Tony Meehan, and the Singing Nun. Unbknownst to me it was also the start of Tamla Motown. Heinz Burt left the Tornados to pursue a solo career as Heinz, and released a single entitled 'Just Like Eddie'. Decades later I can only ponder the question: 'Whatever happened to Heinz?'

Before the year was out, there'd been the Profumo scandal, the closing of Alcatraz, the death of Pope John XXIII, the Great Train Robbery, Martin Luther King's 'I Have A Dream' speech and the assassination of John F. Kennedy. I was, of course, oblivious to most of it apart from the shooting of the President. There was no way of escaping that. I was playing table-soccer with John McReynolds when the news came through via the TV. After a brief pause we carried on with our game.

With the advent of Beatlemania, I was inspired to acquire a four-stringed plastic guitar with a picture of Elvis Presley on the headstock. Brushing aside the image of this fading icon, the neck had a nasty crack in it, though this had no bearing on my inability to play it. Years later, it came to my attention that this instrument came with a 'push button auto-chord' attachment which, in my case, had been forcibly removed—hence the crack in the neck. Within a week I could almost play 'Apache' on one string, which was a start, with or without the auto-chord. However, the Shadows just weren't cool any more. They still had greasy hair, unlike the 'Fab Four' who majored in shampoo and hair dryers. They were hip, man.

Within a week I'd arrived at a justifiable conclusion; the Presley guitar was just a bloody toy, a broken piece of junk. Drastic measures were required to quell my frustration, so I took it upon myself to reply to an advertisement in a popular music paper. The offer promised a catalogue of guitars that were:

"Genuine models of both imported and English production, made of specially selected seasoned woods chosen for their tonal qualities and prepared by craftsmen who have spent their lives in the manufacture of fretted instruments."

Today, as a cynical old pro, I'd describe them as:

"Genuine cheap crap aimed at the elementary student or beginner."

However, to an impressionable twelve-year-old, the Bell Musical Instrument Catalogue contained the sexiest bodies I'd cast eyes on since Kim Novak's last film. Black and white shots of the Watkins Rapier 33, the Burns Vista Sonic and the Levin Goliath filled me with feelings of excitement and anticipation, though the prices brought me back down to earth. The aforementioned Vista Sonic, priced at ninety five guineas, was never going to form an alliance with my under-funded piggy bank, so the cheapest electrified guitar in the brochure—the Rosetti Lucky Seven, at fourteen guineas—became the object of my desires.

The legendary triangular-shaped Watkins Dominator amplifier was available for a reasonable thirty-eight pounds and ten shillings, though the Bird Golden Eagle fifteen watt model with reverb, tremolo and optional set of screw-on legs (thirty shillings for a set of four) came in at thirty nine guineas. Low wage-earning guitarists must have spent many a sleepless night worrying about the extra pound notes that in those days featured a very young-looking Queen Elizabeth.

In June that year, the Beatles played at the Astoria Ballroom in Middlesbrough, and I managed to get hold of a ticket. The place was, as expected, full to capacity. Outside the building, the usual cluster of disappointed fans hunted for tickets. An entry in my notebook at the time described the event:

"Before the Beatles came on to the stage, there were two local groups who were quite good, but when the Beatles came on the place went mad. There was a barrier of two rows of chairs and one row of settees, but that did not stop the crowd from surging over and if it had not been for the officials, they would have climbed onto the stage".

Because of the pandemonium around the stage, I beat a hasty retreat to the balcony area where I found a safe spot amid some older fans. The notebook entry summed up my feelings at the end of the evening:

"Although I was nearly squashed in the Astoria, I still managed to see the Beatles and still think they are the best group out," I gushed.

Within a few weeks I replaced my plastic Elvis Presley guitar with something marginally superior, though inevitably second-hand.

A Plectrum Too Far

Greenwoods the Pawnbrokers stood on a busy, grimy road close to the town centre, and a short walk from the rows of two-up, two-down Victorian cottages, whose dreary facades breathed in the damp air from the murky depths of the River Tees. Ships from all corners of the globe would stop off here to deposit cargo and social diseases before returning to the cold North Sea and all points anywhere. Towering above, less than a mile away, stood the world famous Transporter Bridge, straddling the water like a huge Meccano dinosaur, evoking times of hard work and poverty. I'd heard stories about the dockside area of town and usually managed to avoid it unless my dad took me there on one of our bicycle excursions.

'This is where I used to live, lad,' he reminisced. 'Aye, our house is gone now. By 'eck, times were 'ard. Slag 'eaps and nutty slack.'

What? I glanced about me.

The Gods had definitely not smiled down on this lugubrious place. Swarthy types, presumably from the boats, shuffled about in small groups, smoking heavily and planning, no doubt, another night of licentious activity before setting sail once more for some distant land.

When we dismounted, Dad offered me some advice.

'Watch where you're walking son, you'll get your shoes all clarty (muddy).'

A little later he spoke again, this time without the use of colloquialisms.

"ere, give us a hand, lad,' he said, as he emerged from an alleyway, struggling with a First World War motor car hand pump and an old bicycle frame.

Diplomacy prevented me from enquiring into the logic behind such behaviour, but I had the distinct feeling that my birthday would herald a hybrid biped.

Any thoughts I'd harboured of acquiring a second-hand guitar from Hamilton's music store were soon dispelled as we came to a halt under the three brass balls of the pawn shop. My father had finally succumbed to my constant requests for a guitar and agreed to help me find a cheap one, providing of course, that I mastered the instrument sufficiently to give Segovia a run for his pesetas. My imagination began to run wild. Just what would I be holding close to my chest later that evening? Would I look like a member of a beat group? Would it match my Beatle jacket?

As we entered, the sheer volume of articles packed into one room was overwhelming. Accordions hung breathlessly amongst radio sets, vacuum cleaners, false teeth, treasures of taxidermy, furniture, clocks (which all seemed to strike the hour, every minute) and complete sets of Arthur Mee's *Childrens' Encyclopaedia*. Against the back wall loomed a ceiling-high pile of clothing; no doubt mostly procured from the houses of recently deceased pensioners. Judging by the general disarray, there was a possibility that the remains of one or two of the poor sods were still in there. I half-expected to see Albert Steptoe and Private Frazer from *Dad's Army* arguing the toss over some fingerless gloves.

The place was very musty; now that's a good old English expression— one that can be applied to a frenzied elephant or a new, unfermented wine. Anyway, the gloomy atmosphere suddenly brightened as I spied (with my little eye) a couple of acoustic guitars hanging side by side from the ceiling, like dead Mexicans in a Serge Leone spaghetti western. As the slinky looking electric model that posed smugly nearby had a frightening asking price of fifteen guineas, the dead Mexicans were looking a more realistic buy.

I chose the one with a butterfly motif, naively ignoring the fact that the strings stood roughly one and a half inches above the fingerboard, thus rendering the instrument more suitable for slicing cheese or garrotting hamsters, ensuring my novice fingers were to suffer for some time to come. Dad lowered the instrument from its gallows and studied it like a man who knew even less about guitars than his son did.

"ow much?' he enquired, holding up the object of my desire like a dead rabbit.

'Three quid, mate,' responded the shifty-looking assistant. Dad winced, then scratching his chin, took a sharp intake of breath.

'Two pounds ten—I'm not daft y'know,' he announced. The shifty sod behind the counter looked as though he'd just been offered five bob for his sister.

'Oh, I don't know, first class instrument that,' he remonstrated. 'Tommy Steele played one just like it. 'e went from rags to riches and 'e went to sea when 'e was fifteen.'

My heart began to beat a little faster, as visions of me sitting at home that night caressing the guitar of my dreams began to fade. Dad scratched his cap and stared out of the window. He was not going to concede.

'All right, all right,' conceded Shifty, muttering obscenities under his breath.

He prized the money from my benefactor, took one look at the inch and a half-high string action, bit his bottom lip and gave out a nasal snort. The sadistic bastard. He was probably a local guitarist and proud owner of a Gibson Les Paul Custom model with a fretboard action of .005 of an inch.

Lacking any domestic musical influence, apart from the ramblings emanating from "that bloody piano", it soon became apparent that some kind of tutelage would be appropriate. What was required was the *Dick Sadler Complete Guitar Method*, although it looked about as interesting as a book on nuclear physics. I had never been a particularly enthusiastic scholar and as there were no threats of admonishment—e.g. lines, or the dreaded cane—the publication was respectfully ignored. Still, the images of the Beatles and the Rolling Stones stood foremost in my mind and I decided to persevere to the point where I was able to pick out the odd melody, though chords were still a bit of a mystery. A little voice, possibly influenced by my French teacher Mr Hughes said, "Stick at it laddie—don't be a daftie".

French was worth sticking at; as was geography, art and English. Maths, science and technical drawing induced bouts of nausea, though my regular selection for the school team helped ease the situation. At intermediate level, we were sporting colours that were identical to Boro's away kit—white with a red V-neck and sleeve trim. The comparisons stopped there. No stretch of the imagination could detect an Alan Peacock, Ian Gibson or a Mel Nurse amongst us. Our goalkeeper did point out however, that he had the moral advantage over a recent Middlesbrough keeper, one Esmond Million, who was found guilty of match fixing. He never played professional football again, and was last heard of working as a bus conductor for the local municipal service. Afterwards, people tended to refer to him as "the tosser with the daft name".

Ironically, as our own playing field was still not ready for use, we played our home games away from home at Sandy Flats, a council-owned stretch of land in Acklam, one of the nicer parts of Middlesbrough. Whoever had supplied the goalposts must have been set up for life; there were bloody hundreds of them. I wondered if he'd sold them the line-marking paint as well, just to secure that winter holiday in the Bahamas. Saturday mornings at Sandy Flats might have provided an interesting study for any alien reconnaissance ships. Swarms of puffing schoolboys pursuing a small brown dot across the wide, open spaces of an industrial town suburb, with the general view of giving it a good kick, would probably have persuaded any extra-terrestrials that the time was not yet right to make contact. Phone home? More like let's bugger off home as soon as possible.

Distractions are always helpful, but the reality of exams loomed. GCEs, CSEs and all the other E's (of the educational variety) sounded ominous. As far as I was concerned, they were almost two years away, so why worry? School did have its advantages though, especially the sporting facilities as I was still cracking them into the back of the net for the school team. The playground was an ideal place to discuss the possibilities of forming a 'beat group' with other classmates. Though the majority couldn't distinguish a crotchet from a hatchet, two or three adventurous individuals seemed to be tuned in to the same frequency as me. I suggested that we should bond over lemonade and sweets at my place.

One of my closest schoolmates was John Rowney, an amiable, albeit pasty-looking lad who lived with his folks on the same housing estate as myself. A friendship blossomed through shared tastes; pop music obviously, but also humour and limited fashion-wear. He'd managed to acquire a cap from C&A that bore a striking resemblance to the one worn by John Lennon on The Beatles' conquest of the United States. It offset my round-collared Beatle jacket to a tee. His parents, succumbing to continuous demands for a six-stringed accomplice, had treated their loved one to one not dissimilar to mine. After a few schoolyard enquiries, we discovered that our classmate Paul Rodgers possessed a matching cheap acoustic guitar, and that Dennis Minchella and Ray McConnell would be willing to help out on improvised 'percussion'. Together we entered the world of music with typical schoolboy ineptitude, whilst persuading the other members of the Moody family to retire to the remaining rooms to suffer the ensuing melee.

Oh, to have been a fly on the wall of our dinning room that evening, as the clueless fingers of masters Moody, Rodgers and Rowney, spurred on by a percussive accompaniment (yes, Dennis and Ray hammering the crap out of my mother's pots and pans), strove to put back musical progression by at least three thousand years. Those squeaky monotone voices battling against a wall of tonal ignorance must have given the neighbours some serious thoughts of upheaval.

To uphold the family's standing in the community, my father, desperately trying to escape the youthful carnage, took to trimming the front hedge. As our 'band' attempted a particularly destructive rendition of 'She Loves You', my father told passers-by that the boys responsible for making such a dreadful din were actually imbeciles from a local school for backward children that they were assisting in their plight to overcome social difficulties. As the last discord petered out I concluded that the riff from 'Peter Gunn' was to the guitar what 'Chopsticks' was to the piano. Once again it occurred to me that though my enthusiasm was unchallenged, some kind of musical education was without doubt necessary.

My parents always visited the workingman's club at weekends. It gave my father a chance to down pints at subsidised prices, whilst my mother could enjoy a snowball and watch the evening's entertainment, otherwise known as 'the turn'. One particular Sunday, they returned home extolling the talents of Johnny Goffin, the guitar-playing half of that night's act. Apparently he gave lessons, and aware of my eagerness to progress, had arranged for me to visit him the following Thursday. Thanks! Lying in bed that night, my ambivalent feelings towards the impending private lesson left me tossing and turning to the faint sounds transmitted from a small studio in Luxembourg. I could never figure out why the studios of the coolest radio station on our sets were so far away. Where the hell was Luxembourg, and why, for that matter, did it stay up so late? Didn't its residents have to get up early and work down mines and in steelworks like everybody else? Who was Horace Batchelor and what was an infra-draw method, and why did it all happen at Keynsham (spelt K-E-Y-N-S-H-A-M) near Bristol?

I switched off the radio as well as my brain and went to sleep.

When the big day arrived, my sense of apprehension was so acute, I decided to feign a panic attack at school, but was merely reprimanded for play-acting. By the time I arrived home, the bout of nervousness had morphed into mild stomach cramps. My mother's suggested remedy to my malingering was to recommend swallowing a huge spoonful of syrup of figs. I recovered immediately.

Johnny Goffin was a middle-aged man of middle-age proportions who exuded a seemingly working class snobbery. You know the type, smoked a pipe and read books. Probably had a backyard and owned a lawnmower. Then again he may have been a decent, intelligent man who was being given the once-over by a twelve-year-old council house kid with a rather limited outlook. We were greeted by a haze of St. Bruno pipe smoke and beckoned into his living room. There were items loung-ing in the lounge; furniture, television, bookcase, stuffed hippopotamus etc, but it was the presence of a music stand centre stage that made me want to turn and run out of there. It may well have been a dentist's chair, or an alien being from the planet Zlonc as far as I was concerned. There it was, gazing at me with chromium-plated intensity, hell-bent on my destruction. Somewhere on the periphery of this paranoid state, I could hear Mr Goffin suggesting to my mother that she should come back in forty minutes.

When I removed my starter guitar from the large brown parcel-bag which had acted as a carrying case, I could tell by Mr Goffin's expression that he was far from impressed.

'Hmm,' was his only response, apart from sucking on his pipe.

He then allowed himself a knowing smile before producing something known as a tutor—an instruction book containing what appeared to be diagrams of tadpoles climbing up and down telegraph wires. This, he informed me, was music, and by learning to read it, I could do better than 'all that long-haired lot.' As I happened to be a fan of 'all that long-haired lot', this remark was not appreciated, but I remained passive and let him press on. He then informed me that the *Mel Bay Modern Guitar Method* was the most up-to-date and progressive of all graded guitar courses. By now I was completely lost and seriously considered catching my mother up at the nearest bus stop.

'Right Michael, take hold of your plectrum,' instructed Puffing Billy. Without moving, I shot him a sideways glance.

'You have got a plectrum haven't you?' he enquired.

I patted each of my pockets in turn, hopeful to give him the impression that I may have mislaid one somewhere. He must have fallen for my bluff, because he started to pat his own.

'Here try mine,' he said, handing me something that looked like a toenail shed by someone involved in an industrial accident. I, in turn, held it like one would hold dead body tissue.

'Between the thumb and forefinger, lad, between thumb and forefinger,' instructed the cognisant one.

I gave my hand a studious look, then came to the conclusion that the forefinger must indeed be the fourth or little digit, inspiring me to adopt a pose reminiscent of some arthritic castanet player. He gave me such a despairing look that I could do nothing but smile inanely before dropping the plectrum onto the carpet.

For the remaining thirty minutes, Mr Goffin tried valiantly to persuade one or two of my fingers to press down on the lower registers of the bottom string, an exercise not unfamiliar to him, as he no doubt went through the same motions with other virginal wannabes. I did try, and at one point almost sounded the note of G, but the intensity of the movement caused me to lose my grip on the plectrum and it fell into the sound hole of the guitar. Johnny sat back and scratched around for his weed as the sound of a doorbell ended the first round.

'That'll be your mother,' said Goff the Cough as he hurried towards the door.

'Bloody Hell,' I thought—'the man's psychic!' Maybe if he conducted these lessons by ESP it would cut the travelling costs and insure me against the passive inhalation of Ogden's Nut Ground Shag.

'He's got potential,' enthused Mr Goffin as he prized six shillings out of my mother's wash-dayed hands. 'Oh, and another eight for the tutor book. Same time next week?'

I stepped out from that house like a man who'd just completed a ten year stretch at Wormwood Scrubs, breathing in the freedom of life on the outside. In actual fact, I was inhaling some of the most noxious fumes that the ICI chemical plant at nearby Wilton could produce.

'How was it, son?' enquired a woman who'd just trudged the streets for forty five minutes on my behalf.

'Never again!' I hissed, before going into a sulk.

'It'll be all right,' she reassured me.

How the heck did she know? The only thing she played was Bingo.

Once home, I fondled my security football whilst watching *Crackerjack* ('Crackerjack!'). Five minutes later, my father entered the room and bollocked me in no uncertain terms.

'I didn't spend all that money on that guitar and them flamin' books for nothing, you know. Get practising and be there next week for your next lesson—and you're going on your own too.... I'm flamin' starvin'. Dragging your mother down there with you when she could be at home cooking my dinner. You don't know you're born!'

Honourable though my intentions were, the thought of sitting down for half an hour each day, striking a note and counting to four then repeating it, was not what I had in mind when posing in front of the bedroom mirror a week before. Still, I'd made the commitment, practising for the allotted half hour until I could pick out the three lowest notes with incredibly boring precision.

I readied myself for a brief musical encounter of the second kind.

Friday arrived and I cycled back from school, secure in the knowledge that due to a few hours of finger-slicing fret abuse, I could now face my arbiter with new-found confidence. Even the brown parcel-bag had bitten the dust, thanks to a valiant effort by my mother. Her tailoring talents had produced a made-to-measure carrying bag from material not dissimilar to that of nun's habits. There was every chance that it actually had been, considering that she was an enthusiastic member of the Catholic Women's League. The absence of a handle meant that I had to carry it under my arm. From a distance it must have looked as though I was assisting some inebriated Sister, bereft of limbs, with a two-foot long neck and no head.

On the long walk to the bus stop I attracted the odd inquisitive glance. Twelve-year-old boys do suffer from a certain lack of confidence, some more than others, and the bus stop was a welcome oasis in a desert of self-consciousness.

'What you got in that bag?' a voice interrupted my train of thought.

I gave the young lad a steely glance and turning away, mumbled something about a guitar. Either my muffled response was inaudible, or else the boy was aurally challenged, because he turned to his mate and informed him that I had a 'bucket o' tar' in the bag. I told him to bugger off or I'd kick him in the shins.

'Oh, you will, will ya? Dad, come 'ere.'

A seven-foot tall brute wearing a singlet and boxing shorts stuck his head out of a local pub doorway. I suddenly felt insecure, speechless and erm... shit-scared. Luckily the bus arrived, prompting me to leap aboard clutching my mutilated nun, while Piltdown Man and son took it in turns to shout abuse.

During the lesson, their faces suddenly appeared on the music stave, super-imposed on a pair of quavers. I shivered momentarily. It was the first time I'd quivered over a quaver. Maybe they'd still be there on my return, snacking on raw meat and shooting at cats with an air rifle. On the return journey I hopped off the bus a stop earlier and sneaked home by an alternative route, looking over my shoulder every two and a half seconds.

Class Of '64

In the early Sixties, secondary modern schools employed a form of grad-ing that offered a certain kudos to students of a more academic leaning. Thus, at St. Thomas' Catholic school, the classes A and B were regarded as a technical level. C were those with potential to improve, D sad cases and E were generally encouraged to drink an extra bottle of milk at play-time. I had started my senior education as an A, but by the second year had been relegated to the B stream where, it must be said, I felt more at ease. It was during the 3B period that the 'classroom band' took shape. Though we had some enjoyable evenings demolishing current hits, it soon became apparent that my private musical education, coupled with an inner yearning to be part of a 'proper' group was leaving Dennis and Ray well and truly with the pots and pans. Even though John had per-suaded his parents to buy him a second-hand Hofner Colorama electric, the original 'front-room band' was about to murder its last tune.

As my confidence grew, I was able to convince Mr Goffin that applying myself to elementary guitar was easily within my grasp. Having mastered such musical landmarks as 'Old Black Joe' and 'The Caissons Go Rolling Along', I began to take pride in my ability to 'play properly' and perse-vered with Mel Bay's 'carefully graded, melodious and distinctive method'. This, I was assured, would enable me to perform solos, duets and etudes. Yes, but would it give me the 'beat' like the blokes in groups had? My ever-helpful dad almost came to the rescue when a drinking buddy from his local, the caretaker from a nearby school, offered to coach Paul, John and myself as he'd apparently done with the already established Del and the Falcons. However, learning to play Shadows tunes from sheet music wasn't exactly what we had in mind, and we kicked him into touch after two sessions. It was time for some kind of stimulation. As luck would have it, it wouldn't be too long in the waiting.

Colin Bradley came from an 'elder brother' background, enjoying the shared upbringing of two music enthusiasts, including one who'd shown him some basic chords. He also possessed a Hofner Congress cello-bodied guitar, an instrument of respected vintage on the semi-pro circuit. He'd attended primary school with Paul, and though we'd been classmates for a couple of years, it wasn't till our shared musical interests collided that we became good friends. Following an invitation to his house to have a 'strum' and strip the family larder of anything digestible, we decided to pursue our common ground—beat music. Colin's limited yet impressive repertoire of skiffle hits, Peter Paul and Mary songs, and Buddy Holly covers would need updating, but with my input and recently acquired musical knowledge, and Paul's enthusiasm, there was every possibility of us forming a group.

My primary objective was to upgrade my instrument and having impressed my father with my melodic endeavours had little trouble persuading him to cough up the necessary 'readies'.

'No more than forty pounds though,' he insisted. It sounded like a reasonable offer.

The next few weeks were spent scouring the 'for sale' ads for a suitable replacement, a tedious pastime, but satisfying in the knowledge that soon I'd be plugging in my new guitar with grown-up confidence. Then one evening, the following advertisement appeared in the local newspaper, the *Evening Gazette*:

67. MUSICAL INSTRUMENTS ETC.
For Sale. Harmony Roy Smeck electric guitar.
v.g.c. £42.00. Tel.: M'bro 56843

Persuading my dad to increase his investment by two pounds was a hurdle I didn't even attempt to jump. Optimism would be the key word. Soon I found myself in a phone box pressing button A, nervously enquiring about this 'Roy Smeck' thing.

'Oh it's still 'ere,' uttered the voice at the other end, inspiring me to memorise his address before leaping onto the nearest bus.

Many guitar players, when becoming nostalgic about their instruments, often refer to 'the smell' on opening a mysterious looking guitar case, that exotic blend of mature wood, lacquer and felt, with a hint of passive smoke and steel. I experienced it myself on that evening over four decades ago, and it's something that you never really forget. The instrument looked gorgeous to my impressionable eyes; a creamy butter colour with knobs and chromed grills. I assumed that the latter was for the electric sound. My stomach started to rumble. After a brief musical grope, I nodded my approval and proffered the contents of my trouser pocket as payment, whilst being shrewd enough to leave the pocket lining hanging loose. It hid no more than a few biscuit crumbs and a bent comb.

'Erm, it's forty two actually,' said the man, looking a little hurt by the offer.

'Oh, I've only got this much,' I replied, and gave him a look that a baby spaniel would have been proud of.

Well, he must have been a dog lover because he let me have it! I barked my appreciation but decided to draw the line at licking his face. The journey home seemed timeless and blissful, like walking on air. One happy lad!

Over the next few months I started to get together on a regular basis with Colin and Paul. Mums, dads, brothers, sisters and family pets gave up living room space, often sacrificing their favourite television programmes to support the gallant cause. To make things easier we'd sometimes treat ourselves to the sheet music of current hits. For two shillings and sixpence, schoolboys with a limited knowledge of pop music could scrape through such up-to-the-minute hits as 'Can't Buy Me Love' and 'Things We Said Today' (Beatles), 'Shout' (Lulu), 'I Think Of You' (Merseybeats), and 'Not Fade Away' (Rolling Stones).

I continued with my weekly visits to Johnny Goffin. I convinced myself that this musical education would stand me in good stead, even though the Mel Bay method was a slow, tedious process. The sole requirement was the ability to learn one short piece a week which gave me plenty of time to pursue my pop music interests, undeterred by dotted quarter notes and scale studies in the key of G-Major. As for Mr Bay's arrangement of Hayden's 'Austrian Hymn', it was about as interesting to me as potholing. However, Colin, Paul and myself forged ahead, ignoring not only hymns, but also symphonies, oratorios and a selection of masses also attributed to the great Austrian composer. We'd stick to Mersey Beat, thank you. A neighbourhood friend, Alan Morris, joined up as bass guitarist, but after one or two sessions, it was quite obvious that he wasn't cutting it. He was having difficulties getting the notes into the right order. Eventually, Paul would buy his bass and Alan went on to become a very successful tour manager. What we desperately needed was a drummer.

Q: What is a beat group without a drummer?
A: A folk group, that's what!

Percussionists were definitely in short supply at St. Thomas' that year—not one person with a drum kit! Even the older boys seemed reluctant in their attitude towards self-expression. They just went with the flow. Some of them even went with that fat bird with the unpleasant smell.

Just as we were starting to consider the possibilities of a downward spiral into the world of Peter Paul and Mary, the horrors of 'Puff The Magic Dragon' and 'Stewball' were suddenly dispelled, due to the timely intervention of Barry Usher. He was another lad from the select stream who, on hearing of our dilemma, casually informed us that he was the proud custodian of a Ringo Starr snare drum. Fantastic—now we could be the Beatles! Unfortunately, Barry's snare drum gained more respect than his ability to play it, so he followed Alan Morris into the Museum of Never Was' (maybe he became a tour manager as well). Once again, the spectre of Peter, Paul and Mary loomed ominously.

As in all moments of turmoil, I had a fix of television. This time, the drug of my choice was *The Outer Limits*, a black and white sci-fi series which, to be honest, was pretty scary for its time. Laughable by today's standards, it was a sort of mini B-movie anthology, but to an impressionable Sixties kid, it was the business. Watching the programme for the first time was an unforgettable experience. You're sitting in your armchair, when suddenly the TV flickers into a mass of distorted, wiggly lines. Strange unmusical tones are heard. Just as you get up to give it a whack, a voice declares forebodingly:

'There is nothing wrong with your television set.'

You sit down apprehensively, and the voice continues:

'Do not attempt to adjust the picture. We are controlling transmission. We will control the horizontal. We will control the vertical. For the next hour, sit quietly and we will control all you see and hear.'

Bloody Hell, they've landed!

The doom-laden voice is heard again:

'You are about to experience the awe and mystery that reaches from the inner mind to—*The Outer Limits!*'

A powerful brass section swelled out a huge chord. Badaaaarrr! Once my heart rate returned to near normal, I allowed myself a knowing smile. I turned to my dad who was hiding behind the sofa.

'See, I knew it was only pretending!'

Oh, and the weirdest of weird sounds that was the Theramin! Of course, we never knew what it was till we heard 'Good Vibrations' by the Beach Boys, then the penny dropped.

Music shops have, somewhat unsurprisingly, always played an important part in the lives of musicians; supplying instruments, accessories, recorded works and necessary advice. They've also functioned as meeting places for local band members to discuss a whole range of subjects, notably music and girls. Hamilton's music shop formed an integral part of the town's shopping centre for as long as I could remember; a two-storey building housing both records and musical instruments. The downstairs section offered a comprehensive selection of vinyl records, with small airless cubicles containing a basic turntable and a small speaker for listening to the goods prior to purchase. Fine of course, unless the previous occupant was a cigarette smoking bath-dodger who picked his nose. Wall-bogies at eye level can be pretty disconcerting. Still, we took it all in our stride and added to the ambience by dropping the occasional fart for good measure.

The upstairs dealt with instruments, amplifiers, sheet music, etc. A veritable Aladdin's Cave to the young and impressionable. By now we'd managed to upgrade and had entered the world of amplification. Colin had acquired a pick-up for his Hofner, plus a Watkins Westminster amplifier in nice shades of blue and cream. Paul sported the Vox bass guitar he'd acquired from Alan Morris, though an amplifier was still beyond him. In the meantime he plugged into my recent purchase—a Harmony amplifier (thanks, Dad!). Things were starting to come together.

The focal point at Hamiltons was the display window, where local groups pinned their business cards. Weird, wonderful and soon to be forgotten collectives like the Fly-By-Nights, the Hafta Darks, Del and the Falcons offered up their services. It also served as a 'situations vacant' board for advertising people's rather odd requirements, such as:

Wanted. Blonde-haired rhythm guitarist. Neither mod nor rocker.
Must be rhythmic. Own equipment essential.

This actually fitted Colin's description, but he remained loyal to Paul and myself, probably because he was unsure of his fashion status. We did however observe one postcard of interest, declaring the talents of Malcolm Cairns, a drummer seeking employment within a young musical environment. Colin made contact, and a rehearsal was arranged at a pub near the town centre managed by a friend of my dad. I felt a rush of excitement. The Class of '64 was about to enter the big wide world of show business, in an age when the western world had been presented the freedom of choice the optimistic Fifties promised. Liberation from post-war attitudes had come of age and the younger generation were starting to dive headfirst into an uncharted sea of temerity. The Pill encouraged people to adopt an open mind towards sex, and the music of the day, inspired by the earthy rhythm and blues drifting in from the United States, provided a raunchy accompaniment. Now that the barber's suggestion of "Something for the weekend, Sir?" had become passé, men grew their hair long. In the midst of this orgy of indulgence stood Freddie and the Dreamers, a beat group from Manchester, whose singer resembled a chromosomally-challenged Buddy Holly. Granted, they'd produced a few pop hits, but their image was strictly appalling.

Now, you may be wondering why I've singled out this particular partnership for personal criticism, considering that a few of the older bands had only recently dispensed with Brylcreem, but there is a valid point. Malcolm Cairns looked like bloody Freddie—*qu'elle horreur*!

'This is Malcolm,' announced my dad. 'He say's he's an experienced drummer.' Judging by the buxom girl by his side, there was no doubt about it—he was certainly experienced. We shot sideways glances without moving our heads, which is not easy, then said nothing until the ever-courteous Colin responded with a polite 'Hello.'

Malcolm studied the virginal trio and smiled. He must have thought that, even in the event of musical inertia, he wouldn't have to worry about dragging us out of pubs or brothels. It made us cringe to think we were in the same group as this 'bloke', though to be fair, he hadn't said anything about our cheap schoolboy jeans. Furthermore, he had to be an improvement on Barry Usher and his plastic snare drum. And his bird had tits!

We'd set up our tiny amps in the room upstairs from the bar and waited awkwardly while Malcolm began to assemble his drum kit. Soon, we began to gaze in wonderment at his 'proper drums'. Compared to Master Usher's plaything, it looked like the Taj Mahal standing there proudly in a pokey room in a rough and tumble building in downtown Middlesbrough.

Our living room sessions had stood us in good stead and we were confident enough to suggest the Rolling Stones''What A Shame' to kick off the evening's events. As soon as the opening four bars were under our belts we were off into the unknown, carefully avoiding eye-to-horn-rimmed glasses contact with our first real drummer. It soon became evident that Malcolm was no Charlie Watts, but then likewise, we weren't exactly Keith, Brian and Bill either.

We self-consciously tore through a few more tunes before diving into the ham and pickle sandwiches, allowing ourselves a few moments of rumination before a respectful, albeit rather naive rendition of 'If You Need Me'. Ironically, we needed Malcolm, dodgy image or not, to help launch the musical careers of Mick, Colin and Paul, known collectively as... Ah yes, we'd need a name before we could venture any further.

Oh, and a manager too.

Joe Bradley was a short-distance lorry driver by profession, and Colin's eldest brother. Though there was an age gap of twenty-one years between the two siblings, they had much in common, especially when it came to music. His easy-going, confident personality commanded respect from his male counterparts and exuded a natural charm towards female company; he was definitely a good man to have on board. At Colin's request, he attended the next session, and after listening to a few songs, offered to help us in any way possible. We all knew right away that Joe was the one to help us establish some sort of direction.

What's in a name? Influence, fantasy, ego, fashion or just plain desperation? Speaking as one who has pondered on the subject a few times over the years, I'd say a little of each. Though we'd considered calling ourselves The Premiers, Colin suggested The Intrepids. However, taking the piss out of weak-natured teachers and working with a drummer who looked like Freddie Garrity hardly gave us the authority to be judged intrepid. In the end we settled for The Titans, yet another contradiction in terms. This decision may have been influenced by the front skin on Malcolm's bass drum, which already had the chosen moniker emblazoned across it in rather large letters—a reminder of his previous set-up. I retired that night secure in the knowledge that I was now a member of a fully-fledged beat group who would rise as late as possible to go to boring old school.

I'm A Road Runner, Honey!

Vince Early was our English teacher who, apart from bearing a passing resemblance to B-movie star Darren Nesbit, headed an after-school folk music session for other members of the teaching staff. Colin, as amiable as ever, had sat in one evening, impressing Mr Early with his ability to strum along with their rendition of 'Where Have All The Flowers Gone', whilst enthusing about The Titans and their weekly rehearsals. Vince suggested that we should take the bull by the horns and perform in public, a commendable suggestion considering that Paul's attitude to all things academic had recently taken a turn for the worse. Rebellion was creeping in, and as far as school was concerned, within a year I'd be creeping out.

As 1964 drew to a close, I gave my first public performance, as a member of The Titans at St Mary's Cathedral Hall, Middlesbrough. Mr Early helped set up the venue whilst Paul's elder sister printed up some tickets on her office typewriter. I think admission was two shillings, but we couldn't have cared less—money was not the prime objective. My memory eludes me as to the transport arrangements that cold December night, but assume that Malcolm drove himself, his kit, and ever-present girlfriend to the gig, whilst Joe took care of the three prodigies and their equipment. The expression "PA system" meant nothing to us; we would simply plug two cheap microphones (recently acquired) into our guitar amplifiers and hope for the best. As it turned out, the stage area yielded only one plug socket, and in the absence of any kind of adaptor, two of the amplifiers had to be connected to the mains supply via the overhead light sockets, thus impeding stage visibility to those in the audience.

The ticket sales had fared well, and even Dennis and Ray from the 'Pots and Pans' band lent their support, chatting excitedly with Vince Early, or 'Sir' as he was habitually referred to. Joe helped out where he could, before retiring to the nearest boozer for a quick pint, no doubt enthusing to anybody within earshot about the lads in the hall next door. We busied ourselves by tuning up and parting our hair in the right place until the time came for us to take to the stage. After a certain amount of fumbling about in the dark, I struck a Chuck Berry riff and we were into 'Around and Around'.

We gave it everything we had and managed, as one, to conclude our primitive rendition at roughly the same time, exuding embarrassed smiles towards the appreciative audience. Suddenly, Vince Early appeared at the front of the stage in such an animated state that it looked like curtains for the young rockers after the first ball. We expected the worst. 'Fantastic!' enthused our teacher, as we raised our eyebrows in synchronised surprise. 'Let's have more of the same!'

'Who the 'ell's Morrov The Saim?' assuming it to be a request for an ode to some long-forgotten Viking king.

Receiving a blank look, a suggestion to continue as rehearsed, and another animated leap from our impassioned tutor, we motored head-long into 'Route 66'.

It was a successful night. In fact we were treated to lemonade when we finally ran out of songs. Yep, it was that good.

Mr Early was spot on when he commented that we looked happier on stage than in the classroom. Joe vowed to assist us in our crusade, before driving us back to our proud homesteads to enthuse to our respective parents.

Back at school on Monday morning, resplendent in blazers and grey trousers, the three 'popsters' were granted a little more fuss than usual. The word was out—look out you mop-tops! Soon it would be Christmas, and my presents would hopefully yield some new duds and a Beatle jumper. We would bid farewell to 1964 amidst the sounds of the Rolling Stones (Little Red Rooster); the Supremes (Baby Love); Roy Orbison (Pretty Woman) and Elvis Presley (Blue Christmas), then settle into 1965 with the Beatles (I Feel Fine); Georgie Fame (Yeh Yeh) and the Righteous Brothers (You've Lost That Lovin' Feelin').

Clearly we had much to look forward to.

Friends, Romans, countrymen, lend me your ears—William Shakespeare.
I'm tellin' you mate, they sound great—Joe Bradley.

Once the New Year had sobered up, Joe and his lovely wife Gladys let us use their living room to rehearse, and as a bonus we could listen to records on his stereo radiogram. Wow, what a sound! Gladys would prepare great snacks, and very soon a real family atmosphere prevailed. Not having children of their own, they spoilt us rotten, and of course, we loved it. Joe pointed out that a PA system was of paramount importance, and being the resourceful type, enlisted the services of a friend and neighbour to help us in our quest for sonic self-sufficiency.

Enter Ken Taylor, a thoroughly decent chap who knew more about electronics and engineering than all of us put together. He suggested a practical and affordable set-up consisting of a Leek Variscope mono preamplifier and a Leak TL50 power-amplifier that he would assemble, plus a pair of speaker cabinets, each containing two twelve-inch Fane speakers. Three moderately priced microphones would complete the system, though supporting them came as an afterthought in the shape of mannequin stands 'borrowed' from the gown shop where Gladys was the manager. Malcolm and the schoolboys where ready to rock.

The Titans continued to rehearse, whilst Joe contacted various pubs and workingman's clubs, hard-selling us as "the youngest beat group around", or "R&B at its best". His self-confident and sociable disposition often persuaded landlords and club secretaries to give us a chance. We started to build up our repertoire, which drew heavily on the songs of the Beatles, the Stones, Chuck Berry and other current favourites, as well as Colin's folk, skiffle and Buddy Holly influences.

I still made regular appearances at the court of Johnny Goffin, though the pipe-smoking one was by now approaching his sell-by date. He'd become as boring as school.

It was 1965 and the times they were a-changing. This involved a rapidly maturing testosterone level. Adolescence can be a difficult time of life and it often helps to share these transitional years with others. While Colin, Paul and myself where undergoing a parallel experience, Malcolm, being a few years older, was going off on a different tangent, notably that of a courtship combined with musical indifference.

Joe's persistent visits to local youth clubs and pubs helped secure some initial bookings and introduced our nasal senses to the aroma of stale beer, cheap perfume and cigarette smoke.

Our earliest shows included an audition at the local British Legion Club, where we followed a comedian who finished his set with:

'Oh, you grow your own rhubarb do you? What do you put on it? Manure?

Oh, I usually put custard on mine!'

Our connections within the Catholic fraternity also secured dates at St Mary's Cathedral youth club and a gig at my local St Alphonsus Church hall. I'd volunteered to sing Chuck Berry's 'Talkin' 'bout You', which always seemed to a prompt few sniggers. It was Paul who alerted me to my naive, yet consistent lyrical error. The verse which ends, 'She's so fine, you know I wish she was mine, I get shook up every time we meet', was emerging as, 'She's so fine, you know I wish she was mine, I get stuck up every time we meet'. Oops!

We also did a support spot at the Scene Club, a "groovy" venue that had just played host to the Pretty Things and Wayne Fontana and the Mindbenders. Joe regarded the booking as a good career move and he was probably right. Some of our initial excitement was somewhat dulled though, when one of the bouncers entered the dressing room to use the sink, boasting proudly that his fingers were in need of a wash, due to the fact that they'd "just been up a bird's kilt".

Charming—and I'd just come from six thirty mass as well!

We decided that the band's name was perhaps a little old-fashioned, so it was back on with the thinking caps. We turned to the *New Musical Express* for inspiration. The pages were full of Bob Dylan who was coming to Britain for a sell-out tour. I'd read that the Beatles liked him, which I thought was a bit odd. He was a folk singer wasn't he? Eric Clapton had left the Yardbirds and was to be replaced by somebody called Jeff Beck. Gene Pitney had recorded an album of country duets with George Jones. No inspiration there.

Eventually, we looked to the Chess recordings before deciding on The Road Runners, a progression on the song 'Road Runner' by Bo Diddley. Building up our repertoire was both educational and enjoyable. Our setlist soon boasted such gems as 'Farmer John' by the Searchers, 'What a Shame' and 'Off the Hook' by the Stones, 'I'm A Loser' by the Beatles, plus a selection of hits from the songbook of my favourite artist, Chuck Berry.

On the 17th of March, and with a little help from Mr Early, we performed at our own school dance. To publicise this memorable event, our art teacher, Mr Kominsky, created a hand-drawn poster, which he pinned up in the recreation area. The four of us were depicted in cartoon form accompanied by the following descriptions:

The stupendous fantastic Road-Runners—a top local group comprising Big Bill Bradley, Paul Rodgers (Screaming Lord), Blues Moody, and guest drummer Mad Malcolm Cairns.

Filling out the space were silly little snippets like:

Polish the soles of your shoes before running out—we have no French chalk. Informal dress, please note—knuckle dusters permissible only when wearing gloves. Introducing our own St Thomas' talent—they need the practice! Don't forget—no late transport. The bike shed is at your disposal. No E-types in the bike shed.

To my recollection, the gig was a success. However, on Monday morning we were called to the headmaster's office. He wanted to know why we hadn't offered the night's takings (all six pounds of it) to the school. We explained that we had guitars and amplifiers to pay for and that profit was an unknown commodity in the group. He remained unconvinced and informed us that further performances would not be tolerated. What an arsehole.

Our decision to include a drum solo in the set backfired. Unfortunately, Malcolm's percussive poundings were less than impressive, and continuing with a drum solo was definitely out of the question. In fact, after a few gigs, continuing with the same drummer was out of the question.

We plucked up enough courage to ask Joe to pluck up enough courage to inform Malcolm of our wishes, before slinking off into the night. After the dirty deed was done, we sat down with Joe over a Gladys 'special' to discuss plans for a replacement. Malcolm was understandably gutted by our decision to let him go. The conclusion that we needed another drummer was about as far as we got.

During one of Joe's recce's round the local hops, he befriended a young drummer by the name of Ian Naisbit, who offered to help us out on the two or three gigs. The first engagement was poorly attended, maybe twenty people by the time we were due on stage. I asked the manager if we could delay the start but he declined. 'There's a coach arriving in half an hour,' was his answer.

He was right. When it arrived, they all got in it and cleared off. Halfway through the second gig, which was much better attended, Ian began to sweat profusely.

'Can't you lot play any slow tunes?' he pleaded.

This was food for thought; a bit more light and shade was definitely required. After the gig, we asked our exhausted percussionist, who was steaming like a Derby winner and downing a full pint, if he'd like to join the band. He declined, citing the probability of acute weight loss and prior commitments, but recommended a friend of his, Dave Usher.

As usual, Joe and Gladys gave us the run of their living room to audition our second drumming Usher. We arrived that evening to find Joe sporting a rather amused expression, apparently brought about by his earlier introduction to the somewhat eccentric Dave.

'Well, lads,' he started, 'he's a bit of a character this one.'

The conversation suddenly came to a halt as the doorbell chimed. Enter Dave Usher—exit gasps of disbelief. He looked nothing like his namesake, Barry. In fact he looked like nothing I'd ever clapped eyes on before. His bright ginger hair flowed over his shoulders and down most of his back and face, offsetting his rust coloured Sloppy-Joe jumper with almost surreal effect. Grubby jeans and winkle-picker boots completed a picture of absolute sartorial failure.

'This is Dave,' announced Joe. Muttered responses of 'Allright?' greeted the oddball as we fidgeted with our instruments. The conversation continued in the slightly embarrassed mode as Joe prompted the proceedings by giving Dave a hand to set up his drum kit. In no time at all we were off into beat-groupdom, sounding like we'd never sounded before. Dave was on board and the ship was ready to sail.

I still had a life outside of the Road Runners; football, television, the cinema etc, and according to my diary, I saw both *Goldfinger* and *Dr Terror's House of Horrors* in the same week. My life was becoming just one big social whirl! Then an advert for The Globe in Stockton caught my eye. It was an advert for a "one-showing only" of a rock film called *The T.A.M.I. Show*, which featured live performances by Chuck Berry, The Beach Boys, The Supremes, Jan and Dean, Marvin Gaye, Smokey Robinson and The Miracles, plus the Rolling Stones. Even Jagger and company, then at the height of their popularity couldn't top James Brown's devastating performance, which climaxed with the mesmerising 'cloak and stagger' routine during 'Please, Please, Please'. We eventually filed out into the daylight to await a gradual return to reality. Inspired, I went straight home and practised more Keith Richards' licks.

It soon became clear that we'd need to work on a more regular basis to once again update our equipment. Dave's genuine commitment became immediately apparent by his decision to trade in a seemingly perfect Shaftsbury drum kit for a super deluxe red sparkle Trixon set-up. In retrospect I'd say the reasons for this were purely artistic, but one could have mistaken it as a ruse to detract some of the attention away from his rather bizarre image. He had taken some of his old clothes down to the Oxfam shop but they'd refused to accept them.

Not wishing to be outdone, I took steps to update my rather sad-looking back line of amplification, and aided by heartfelt pleas and part-exchange, managed to acquire a Watkins Pick-a-Back amplifier which looked pretty cool to me. The bookings eventually started to trickle in, and as we weren't in a position to invest in a van (like the big lads), Joe advanced us eight pounds and negotiated a deal on a small trailer. When hooked on to his Consul, it served us well for the time being.

Some people misinterpreted the coincidence that in upgrading our equipment we had all chosen red instruments as a preconceived attempt at early image-building. Image? It would take a hell of a lot of imagination to see beyond what we actually were—three schoolboys and a social misfit.

One thing I've learned over the years is that if you try too hard, you'll almost always fail to get the desired result. So, with regard to image, the age of adolescence is often a period of confusion and inspired individualism which some adapt to better than others. We didn't do too badly I suppose, though it didn't stop us being envious of the older lads who could afford to travel to Newcastle and purchase (or steal) the latest London styles. This sometimes led us to sport some rather sad combinations. I remember being impressed by a pair of grey and yellow dogtooth-check 'hipster' pants worn by The Who's Roger Daltrey, and pestered my mother until she promised to buy me a pair on her Saturday shopping expedition. The excitement rose as I rushed home to try on my new 'duds,' but subsided depressingly when I glanced at the mirror. The reflection showed the top half of a skinny youth, whose bottom half was enveloped by what appeared to be the hindquarters of a jaundiced pantomime horse.

I haven't worn yellow since.

My friendship with Paul Rodgers continued to flourish and we'd often meet in the town centre to wander about, as teenagers do. If we were feeling particularly mischievous, and if there were enough of us, we'd act out a mass wind-up. Our most successful required four or five of us to stand on the pavement outside Binns, Middlesbrough's most prestigious department store. Once positioned, we'd look up towards the top floors of the building with the kind of concerned expressions as if expecting an ominous event. Pointed fingers and gasps of disbelief added a touch of authenticity to our anxious stares. In no time at all, our little group began to swell with curious bait-takers.

Back on the school front, some bright spark of a teacher who'd spent some time in America, decided that it would be fun to get the entire class to write to another bunch of sitting ducks over in the Colonies, and bequeath upon them the title 'Pen Pals'. I wrote to a certain John Annal in Syracuse, New York State, describing in a simple, honest manner, how the people from a working class environment in Middlesbrough went about their daily lives. A month latter, I received a letter from him informing me that 'Our houses are nothing like yours. We live in single houses. They are much bigger than yours. We have front porches, cellars, upstairs, screen doors and many other things that you don't have'. I toyed with the idea of replying, mentioning a few things that we did have, such as a monarchic heritage, Shakespeare, the Beatles and the Pilgrim Fathers, plus good manners and social graces, but came to the conclusion that he was just a tosser and threw his nauseating correspondence into a corner. My mother obviously found it because it turned up again amongst a bunch of old press cuttings and memorabilia that I'd compiled to assist me during the writing of this book.

Where is he now? I bet he never made it as a rock star. Considering his improbable name, perhaps an Up yours! is appropriate for John Annal.

Joe organised the printing of some business cards, and soon the Road Runners were pinned up alongside our peers in Hamilton's window. He accepted bookings at Whinneybanks Youth Club, the Blytholme Social Club (where my Auntie Hilda worked as a barmaid), and the Catcote Hotel over in West Hartlepool. These and other exotic establishments were the beginnings of my musical career. I lived for the next gig, the latest record releases, and my mam's Panacalty, (Northumbrian stew consisting of corned beef, carrots and onions bathed in a sea of gravy). Complications were for old blokes in their twenties.

Choosing my next guitar was a very simple and straightforward exercise. All that was required was a dad with some money and a limited knowledge of mid-priced electric guitars. The shape of the thing was of the utmost importance, and as Keith Richards played an Epiphone

Casino, my preference lay in that direction. Burdons in Stockton had in their display window a Harmony H77 model similar in shape to the revered Mr Richards' instrument, but in red as opposed to sunburst. The Teesside area seemed to be bestowed with Harmony equipment, and eventually two guitars and one amplifier were fated to come into my possession. Anyway, I accepted the alternative tint and was offered a part-exchange value of twenty five pounds on the Harmony Roy Smeck, an offer which did not impress my father as he had to fork out sixty five pounds to complete the deal.

'There's nothing wrong with that one. What do you want to change it for?'

'Because this one looks like Keith Richards' guitar. Because it'll improve my standard of playing.'

'Well, I hope so. I'm not a bloomin' millionaire, you know.'

I was happy that I was one more step forward in my musical career. Two days later, on the 12th of June 1965, the guitar, held proudly by its new owner, made its Road Runners debut at St. Chad's church hall, Middlesbrough—where we played non-stop for two-and-a-half hours! By the time we reached the final song, our fingertips were almost bleeding. From then on, Joe took pity and lugged an 80lb Truvox reel-to-reel tape machine around with him to ensure that the kids would be occupied during breaks.

This, he assured us, would "prevent boredom and fights breaking out".

Our bookings at the time were secured by our newly acquired mentor, courtesy of a type-copied circular which went as follows:

THE ROAD RUNNERS

Dear Sirs,

It gives me pleasure to convey to you the following information
'THE ROAD RUNNERS' Rhythm Group is comprised of Lead, Rhythm and Bass Guitar, Vocals and Harmonica and Drums.

We have recently played, with success in most local Youth Clubs, also a number of Social Clubs and Institutes on Tees Side and in the South Durham Area.

We have a number of future bookings on Tees Side, but at the moment we are "not busy". It would give our group pleasure to be considered for a booking at your establishment.

Our fee is negotiable, depending on the distance to travel and the type and length of performance require and whether a weekday or weekend.

Enclosed is a stamp addressed envelope, but if you wish to telephone, a call to the above-mentioned number, between 6.30 and 9.0 p.m. will receive our prompt attention.

I am Sir,

Yours respectfully

J. Bradley. (Manager)

Rhythm group—what a lovely expression! I suppose we'd have been happier with Rhythm and Blues, a burgeoning influence attributable mainly to Dave Usher. He'd acquired a handful of EP's on the Chess-Pye International label featuring Howlin' Wolf, Tommy Tucker, Buddy Guy and Little Walter. We were duly impressed. Chuck Berry obviously didn't have the monopoly on the label, even though our set-list soon gave us the option on no less than seventeen of his compositions. However, we were unable to approach the Howlin' Wolf tunes with the required enthusiasm, as our powers of emulation regarding huge black men from Mississippi were rather limited. Instead, we persevered with our Hollies, Kinks, Stones and Merseybeat, realising correctly that we'd have plenty of time to get the blues when we were older.

If I was asked to name two people who created the greatest impression on me as a teenager, I'd have no hesitation in citing Spike Milligan and Jeff Beck. As my dad was not a fan of *The Goons*, I was never really aware of their radio series in the late fifties and very early Sixties. I had to wait for the *Telegoons* before I would succumb to Milligan's devastating sense of humour. I was a lot luckier with Beck who I got to see at the Kave Dwellers Club in Billingham just after he had joined the Yardbirds. Now here was a man who was more than a mere guitar virtuoso—he was a showman to boot. Stepping into Eric Clapton's shoes had to be a daunting task, not literally as I'm sure the pioneering Mr Clapton's taste in footwear stopped somewhat short of desert boots! However, from the ankles up, Beck's playing and on-stage presence was truly remarkable. An influential night and a great source of inspiration to an impressionable youth.

Jeff Beck wasn't the only eye-catching feature that night. Testosterone, hormones and probably other kinds of 'ones' were also out in force. Rick Derringer once recorded a song entitled 'Guitars and Women' which included the lines: "Guitars and Women, they both need that tender touch, Guitars and Women, they cost and they take so much". Originally the comparisons were derived purely from the shape and contours of the traditional Spanish instrument, which possessed a certain pseudo-romantic pointer towards the female form. These lustful observations were later dashed due to the introduction of electric solid-bodied things that the majority of us now employ. However, in my opinion, guitars are definitely sexier than drum kits (and pianos, accordions, banjos, sitars, trombones and tubular bells for that matter). Maybe I'm just biased.

Christine from Roseworth Youth Club bore no resemblance whatso-ever to my red Harmony. She was a nice looking lass whose appearance near the stage one night stole my attention and stirred my loins, distract-ing me until a break between sets gave me an opportunity to cast one of my shy smiles in her direction. Paul joined me and chatted up her friend as me and Christine made awkward small talk. We arranged to see each other a couple of days later, but after two or three treks around the locale, we mumbled our farewells and parted. I think we saw each other again, but inexperience and self-consciousness prevented any dormant sexual feelings surfacing, so I went home to my Harmony H77.

You Call It—We'll Play It

No more latin, no more french, no more sitting on a hard board bench—anon.

I confirmed my non-committal attitude to the school authorities by refusing their kind offer of GCSE examinations. Another year at school was about as appealing as a holiday in Scunthorpe. The headmaster, a nasty piece of work called Mr Docherty, who was still smarting from the Road Runners school gig, called me to his office.

'Do you realise what you're doing, laddie?' he barked.

'Yes, sir,' I replied.

'You're going to go out into the big, wide world with no qualifications whatsoever?' he continued.

Correct, you bald-headed bullying bastard, I wanted to reply, but, 'Yes, sir,' was all I could manage.

'In that case, why not spend your last few weeks out on the playing field,' he suggested. Great, I thought. Girls in shorts etc. I got up to leave.

'Oh, and while you're there,' he concluded, 'take a big cardboard box and pick up every stone and pebble on every inch of grass.'

Yes, then when it's full I'm going to come back here and shove it right up your arse.

Of course, I never had the pleasure.

My search for a cardboard box never materialised. What could he do—expel me? I'd be out of his hair (or should I say scalp) a month later, so why should I care? This attitude gained me a certain amount of credibility in the classroom, and a girl called Ann, who'd been to a couple of Road Runners gigs and made advances towards me. We met as part of a crowd a few times, but apart from the odd snogging session, the relationship went no further. She was a bit too racy for a sensitive boy like me and I fired her enough blanks to marshal a sports day. She eventually got the message. Anyway, there were plenty more fish in the sea, as they say.

The school leavers department arranged for me to be interviewed by British Steel, in the vain hope of acquiring a position in their technical drawing department. No chance, young man—not enough CSEs. In fact, no CSEs! In the end I was offered an apprenticeship in motor mechanics at a local garage and decided to take it. My parents were pleased. I had a "job with a future, lad", and a whole month beforehand to find a cardboard box and be a Road Runner. So, in July 1965, at the ripe old age of fourteen years and eleven months, I gave my final performances as a schoolboy, entertaining the patrons of such high-profile establishments as the Acklam Steelworks Club; Joe Waltons Youth Club; Saint Mary's College and the Catcote Hotel, West Hartlepool. We were well received at most venues, or lived to play another day, apart from the Acklam Steelworks Club where we were paid off for being too loud. Loud? We only had 25-watt amplifiers, for God's sake!

John McCoy's Crawdaddies were regarded as *the* band in the Middlesbrough area. Fronted by the charismatic McCoy, they'd evolved into a hip soul band that wore Ivy League jackets and had played in London. These credentials were impressive at the time. The Road Runners were booked as the support act one night, and bathed in the exiting atmosphere that a big crowd created. The Crawdaddies and their roadie, Howard 'Maz' Mayes, were very kind to us and by the end of the night, John offered us all honorary membership to his club, Mr McCoys. This proved to be a noble gesture, for over the ensuing eighteen months, we spent many memorable nights there, grooving to the latest soul releases or, more importantly, catching the live acts. The Who and Stevie Wonder were amongst the big stars that we were lucky enough to see, as well as club-circuit favourites like Zoot Money's Big Roll Band, Steam Packet (featuring Long John Baldry and Rod Stewart), the Brian Auger Trinity, and Jimmy James and the Vagabonds. I don't know how the staff was recruited, but hereditary madness and a degree in piss-taking must have been essential requirements.

Big Lenny was the chief bouncer at Mr McCoys for obvious reasons; he was a big, mean looking, bald-headed man with a face like Napoleon in the cartoon version of George Orwell's *Animal Farm*. A definite put-off for would-be troublemakers.

The similarity didn't stop there. He once went to a fancy-dress ball as Porky the Pig where he won first and second prize. All in all, a good enough motive for patrons of the club to behave in a reasonable manner.

His day job was that of a butcher in one of the rougher parts of town, where he would idly pass the time of day hacking carcasses into sizes consistent with a shopping bag. His regular clientele, oblivious to fat-free diets and vegetarian cuisine, would sometimes forgo their regular demands for sausages and chops and request orders of an almost savage nature. One such requirement was for a pig's head, a reasonable request by anyone's standards, except maybe the pig. The necessary phone calls were made, and a pig's head was delivered that night to our *agent de viande* at Mr McCoys nightclub. The item, delivered in a sack, was accepted and stored away till closing time. Walking home and carrying the sack over his shoulder, Lenny was approached by the local beat bobby, which inspired a conversation of almost vaudevillian repartee:

> POLICEMAN: *'What's that you've got on your shoulder, Lenny?'*
> LENNY: *'A pigs head.'*
> POLICEMAN: *'Yes, I know, but what's in the sack?'*

At Lenny's funeral, the mourners were shocked by the inscription on his tombstone. It read: 'What are you looking at?'

Displaying a somewhat mellower outlook, the other doorman, Terry 'Tessa' Davidson had a persona owing more to actor Jack Smethurst than Vlad the Impaler. His cheeky face was usually encountered at the entrance of Mr McCoys in his official capacity, though he would sometimes be required to man the cash register. When employed in the latter role, his lack of height was even more noticeable due to the vertically enhanced cash desk. The paying customer was afforded only a view of his head and shoulders (just visible through a cloud of tobacco smoke), a pair of arms and a glimpse of tie. What went on behind and beneath the 'jump' was open to discussion. There were rumours of obscured sexual activity which, if true, would pre-date Bill Clinton's antics by decades. He also had an annoying habit of starting sentences with 'Ee, aye' or 'Oy, you!' Pressurised into seeking help for this condition, he paid a visit to the doctor who diagnosed his patient as suffering from "Irritable Vowel Syndrome". Given the fine line between truth and legend, it's fair to say that Tessa was probably a victim of both.

The Road Runners set-list continued to expand to incorporate a folk spot, inspired initially by Colin's folk and skiffle roots. We added a few trendy Bob Dylan tunes plus Donovan's 'Catch the Wind' to become an outfit specialising in the ability to slip into 'versatile' mode. This inspired Joe to have some business cards printed bearing the slogan:

YOU CALL IT—WE'LL PLAY IT.

Thanks, Joe. When some of the local piss-takers got wind of our confident boast, they responded with shouts of "'Take Five' by Dave Brubeck," and "Dominique', you know, by the Singing Nun!' Even Bach's 'Gavotte in D-Minor' got thrown at us one night, but we managed to escape by claiming that we only recognised the original version in C-Major, and that Bach never played any of our tunes, so why should we play any of his? Sometimes the audiences were hard and unresponsive, at others warm and encouraging; you learned to take the rough with the smooth, though when they were rough, man, they were rough!

I chose to sing Chuck Berry's version of an Eddie Jones' song called 'The Things That I Used To Do (Lord I Don't Do No More)', a slow blues that dealt with the pain of lost love. Not entirely in a position to empathise with the lyric, the only things I was "doin' no more" was playing football in the road, going to bed early, and wearing short trousers in the summer. Heartache, anguish, and misplaced passion would come later.

Being so young did have its advantages. We avoided getting beaten up by cretins who thought we were trying to pull their birds. Some of the older bands were regarded with a certain amount of animosity for prancing about and eyeing up the local talent. On more than one occasion the dressing room door was pushed open by big lads looking for trouble. Their aggression was immediately dispelled at the sight of neat looking schoolboys studiously tuning their instruments and eating crisps.

Sometimes we would be greeted by some moron at the bar in a workingman's club, guzzling his pint with all the gusto of a dog licking its balls.

'Look at that daft twat,' he'd say in a loud voice commentating on Dave's long ginger locks.

His accompanying pond-life would laugh. We didn't.

Our next door neighbours showed no such hostility the night I was being dropped off after a gig. A party that was in full swing as I was collared carrying my guitar towards my front door.

'Come on, you and the other lads, get your gear in 'ere and give us a tune!' commanded an intoxicated Mr Hinchcliffe.

I can only assume that we were too polite to refuse, as the full compliment of equipment ended up in that small council house. The amps and P.A system were placed in front of the living room fireplace, and due to lack of space, the drums ended up in the dining room. After three songs the police arrived following complaints from half the neighbourhood. There should be a blue plaque on the wall of that house:

MEMBERS OF FREE, BAD COMPANY AND WHITESNAKE
PERFORMED HERE, SUMMER 1965.

The entertainment for workingmen's clubs was decided on by a 'committee'. These were often deluded types who couldn't decide if they were do-gooders or good-doers. The most prominent member would often assume the role of Master of Ceremonies. This then entitled him to abuse the microphone with belts from his hand and blows from a Senior Service-scented breath. The position also required him to provide the audience with both continuity and a modicum of common sense. It also necessitated the administration of the raffle, a straightforward enough exercise in anybody's estimation, though there were exceptions.

The M.C. at the Ironopolis Club in Middlesbrough once announced that the evenings star prize was 'six lovely grills'.

'Did 'e say girls?' enquired one confused soul.

The answer was obviously no, as he proffered six cardboard plates containing a selection of curled up raw meats and feathery-shelled eggs. In the 'men's bar', a group of rough-looking blokes sat at a table playing dominoes.

Dominoes, I ask you! Well, it was hardly Dodge City was it?

The summer months saw bookings in pretty North Yorkshire market towns such as Brompton and Richmond, where we performed in the grounds of the old castle. On one of these gigs, an older lad from the headline act complimented me on my playing, but suggested that the task would be made a lot easier if I fitted my guitar with lighter-gauge strings. Ah, now he tells me! The secret, apparently, was to dispose of the wound third and replace it with the second string, which was made of plain steel. Then, simply add another first in place of the re-located second. Voila! Suddenly my fingers were on a holiday of a lifetime, for a lifetime.

This enlightened state led me to an intense period of 'bending-madness' where the continual pushing up and down of guitar strings caused my calluses to develop calluses of their own. The novelty wore off eventually, allowing familiarity to add some method to the madness. I'm still indebted to that fellow, whoever he was.

A Proper Job

It's true hard work never killed anybody, but I figure why take the chance?
— *Ronald Reagan.*

I became an employed person two weeks before my fifteenth birthday, which probably wouldn't happen these days due to stricter laws on child labour; but where there's muck there's brass. As an apprentice motor mechanic it was definitely a case of more muck and grease than brass. The proprietor, a Mr Newson, introduced me to the two senior mechanics, and one of them, a nice fellow called Brian, gave me a quick guided tour round the greasy work shop. Before he'd finished, he related a little story to me: 'A bloke brought his car in last week complaining about the bad smell coming through the air vent. I took the system to bits but couldn't find anything wrong, so I put the car on the hoist and had a look underneath. I soon found the cause—do you know what it was?' I told him that I didn't have a clue. 'The remains of a dead dog that was jammed behind the axle,' he replied.

Nice start.

My initial given task was to scrape the workshop floor with a blunt tool, a straightforward enough exercise hampered only by the fact that the previous person for this job preceded me by about twenty years. The blisters that eventually appeared on my hands after a few hours gave me serious concern regarding the next gig. Perhaps the Road Runners would be the first act to feature a guitarist who performed the entire set with his toes, whilst stinking of Castrol engine oil. Fortunately, the arrival of a pair of industrial gloves on the second day prevented any such spectacle.

Oh, the oil, the oil!

If they'd put a match to my dungarees that week, I'd have gone up like a suicidal Buddhist monk.

And the pay, the pay!

Two guineas a week for five-and-a-half days of toiling under the critical glances of Mr Newson. I suppose he was giving me a chance to earn myself an apprenticeship, but my initial enthusiasm started to wane after a few weeks.

I just wanted to rock and roll.

I met my nemesis a month later when I unfortunately forgot to tighten up the nuts on a complete set of new wheels I'd just fitted to a test-drive car. The poor prospective customer only got as far as the Town Hall, when three of them parted company with the chassis, resulting in a scene reminiscent of a Laurel and Hardy film. The first one rolled off down Corporation Road, the second struck a passing milk float, whilst the third, obviously enjoying the premature thrills of an early retirement, bounced as far as the Royal Infirmary hospital before sidling to a halt in the middle of the outpatients department. Mr Newson gave me my notice and to be quite honest, I didn't give a damn. My mother assured me that it wasn't the end of the world. Mr Newson probably disagreed.

Early retirement had its advantages. I could lie in bed until midday, eat a cooked lunch (or dinner as it was then called), play my guitar and listen to records. Why get up at some unearthly hour, administer self-inflicted injuries and end up covered in shit for a measly pittance? I could be a Road Runner and a lazy bastard and still earn as much money as an apprentice motor mechanic. Unfortunately my father disagreed.

'How long d'you think these groups will last?' he would ask, before accusing me of being pig-headed.

'Get yourself another apprenticeship—you'll be set up for the rest of your life.'

I journeyed to the job careers building with all the enthusiasm of a vegetarian entering an abattoir. On the way, I cheered myself up by purchasing my favourite magazine *Beat Instrumental*, the only monthly publication to gain the respect of both professional and amateur musician. It featured articles on all the latest 'Beat' sensations, news on all the latest gear, and regular columns such as Player of The Month.

In the autumn of 1965 I finally bade farewell to Johnny Goffin's weekly guitar lessons and said hello to a new career as an apprentice heating engineer. My new boss was a mole-like creature called Don Fisher, flat cap and all. I had no real problem settling in, though rising early on a cold misty morning was, and still is, a real effort. Central heating, though in its infancy, was the new luxury. Don obviously had it sussed, but donkey jackets and steel-toed boots never really figured in my future plans. Once again, it looked like I was on a hiding to nothing. My feelings of discontent were stretched even further by one of Don's employees, a porcine-featured idiot called Arthur, whose period of National Service seemed to have left him permanently scarred. He managed to alleviate some of his angst by intimidating fifteen-year-old boys such as myself.

'You'll never make anything of yourself if you don't liven yourself up,' he'd pontificate. 'I bet you've been playing with yourself all night.'

Of course, he didn't speak to his peers in the same manner. Instead, he regaled them with tales of his sexual exploits during his enforced stint in the army. I assumed by their approving nods and winks that the other tradesmen on the sites were impressed with his apparent libidinous behaviour. Not so, apparently.

'What a wanker!' remarked an electrician with a knowing smile.

'Bullshitter!' came a voice from another room.

I allowed myself a quick snigger and headed for the toilet.

My future as a plumber was curtailed after seven weeks, after which I opted for a job at Millets, those well known purveyors of work and leisure attire. They sacked me after three days, claiming that I "expressed a negative attitude towards salesmanship". How pompous! Didn't they realise that it's almost impossible to negotiate a sale of industrial-strength socks when your thoughts are emotionally engrossed in a Buddy Guy solo?

No, so to Hell with them—*viva Les Road Runners!*

I celebrated my liberation by purchasing a second hand Vox AC 30 amplifier, and within a few weeks we said goodbye to the trailer when Joe found us an old Bedford Dormobile van. It was to serve us well, like a faithful old horse whose awareness of the inevitable knackers yard inspired it to chug on till it dropped. Dave, with a determination that was to be commended, took his driving test and passed first time, enabling Joe to cruise to the gigs at leisure.

Our band started to attract a small fan base; just a few local lasses who thought we were cute. As one or two of them were quite passable in the looks department, we would often exchange small talk and flirtatious banter. A few of them even made up a banner from an old sheet, which expressed their love for us in red paint:

PAUL, MICK, COLIN, DAVE—WE LOVE YOU!!

Though it did wonders for ones' self-esteem, it failed to make an impression on the judges at the Darlington Civic Theatre's annual talent contest. A blind piano player beat us into third place—and it wasn't Ray Charles. We played 'Get Off My Cloud', the Stones' latest hit, and in the front row were these two horrors from Stockton who we'd always try and avoid. The better looking of this duo was just plain ugly, whilst her friend was so repulsive that I christened her The Mutant, a term gleefully acknowledged by the others. If I was pushed into making a comparison with The Mutant, I'd plump for one of the Aquaphibians off *Stingray*, though their master, the evil Titan, ruler of Titanica, would have been shocked that one of his ocean menaces could have even been considered as a lookalike. They would follow us around like pantomime hyenas, waiting to pounce at any opportune moment. Fortunately, their possessiveness was to be their undoing one night, when the least repellent of the two flew into a jealous rage and attacked a rather attractive new fan, reducing her to tears. Joe, voicing all our opinions, warned the pair of them to keep their distance at any future gigs. We never saw them again. During moments of acute boredom, coupled with some sort of perverse curiosity, I've tried to imagine what The Mutant looks like now, but the images conjured up have been too frightening to contemplate.

As Christmas approached, the band's itinerary expanded with traditional seasonal bookings more commonly known as 'Work's-Do's'. At one of these occasions, Dave, suffering from a heavy cold, remedied his affliction with regular slugs from a bottle of Veno's cough medicine. By the time we took to the stage, the entire contents were working their way round his system. Halfway through the second number there was an almighty crash, not unlike the sound of a red-headed percussionist rendered unconscious by liquid chloroform collapsing onto a drum kit. We turned around to witness Dave's admission to the Club A Gone-Gone. It signalled the end of an extremely short first set.

Joe was first on the scene, indicating that we should lend a hand in returning Dave to a more dignified position—the dressing room. Being completely zonked, he looked like he was doing an impression of a new-born baby deer. He was in no condition to walk to his drum kit, let alone play it. Within minutes, there was talk among the punters that, like all pop musicians, we were on pills and hemp, but our rider of fizzy drinks and potted beef sandwiches soon dispelled any suspicious thoughts that they may have been harbouring. Paul and myself, always the jokers, took to cupping our hands to our mouths and shouting, 'Is there a drummer in the house?' The answer was no, but if we required a filing clerk, there were over two hundred of them in the main lounge. The head of the committee panicked. He was a tall, thin man with a huge hooked nose and a bald head who resembled a Gryphon in an off-the-peg suit.

'What yer goin' t'do?' he asked with a bird-like twitch of the head.

'Don't worry,' responded Joe, 'we'll sort something out.'

Terry Popple, already an established drummer with The Phantoms, came to our rescue after Joe's hasty telephone call. Luckily, he lived close by, and within half an hour he was up behind Dave's kit, busking his way through our set with commendable verve and a winning smile. The filing clerks shaked and shimmied the night away and another 'do' was done. The following night, with Dave still incarcerated, Terry joined us for another Christmas party, this time at John Collier's clothes factory. We faced a large crowd of wanton females and it was not a pretty sight.

Somehow we all managed to escape at the end of the night with our virtues still intact; no mean feat considering the reputations of some of their employees. Joe, together with a young, burly workmate called Dave Gray, managed to keep waves of fearsome women from dragging us away to their scented lairs.

(Terry and I would work together again in more permanent circumstances with both Tramline and Snafu.)

The same week, with Dave back behind the drum kit, we played St. Mary's restaurant—yes, the very same place where the Moodys had enjoyed their subsidised Saturday lunches. Joe had managed to persuade his employers, Crossley's Brick Company, to let the Road Runners play support to Mike McGill, frontman of the now defunct McGill Five. Halfway through our set, I noticed that Joe was having a heated conversation with some half-cut individual who, judging by his gesticulations towards the stage, was not entirely happy with our performance. The pair moved into the small dressing room, which had an open doorway leading on to the stage, from where they could be clearly seen, pushing and shoving each other until the inebriated one went for our manager by the throat. Joe, obviously recognising the looks of concern on our faces, mouthed the instruction to 'Keep on playing—the show must go on,' before catching his attacker with a left hook. The show went on, as rehearsed.

On another occasion, a friend's group was playing support to a dance band, when a drunkard approached the stage from the back of the hall, trying desperately to wend his way with some semblance of dignity. When he finally reached his destination, he waved at the bandleader for attention.

'Do yer play requests?' slurred the inebriate.

'What would you like to hear?' replied the man in charge.

The drunkard's face took on a look of complete bewilderment. He stared blankly at the bandleader for a while, then, in an effort to justify his motive replied, 'Anything!'

A most memorable encounter took place a few days later during a Christmas dance for the staff of our old school, St. Thomas'. I have a feeling that Vince Early was instrumental in booking the band, offering us the same enthusiastic encouragement he'd shown during our debut performance. Paul, unlike me, had had the good sense to secure a couple of CSEs prior to his leaving school. Halfway into our well-received set, our ex-headmaster, the despotic Mr Docherty, appeared in front of us.

'Turn it down, it's too damn loud!' he remonstrated.

Dave, oblivious to his identity, laughed out loud, whereas Colin, who still had some months to go at school, looked decidedly uncomfortable. Before I had a chance to express my feelings, Paul stepped forward to put him in his place.

'Why don't you piss off!' he suggested.

'You can't talk to me like that, Rodgers,' countered the domineering one. I looked around for a cardboard box to shove up his arse, our last encounter still fresh in my memory.

'Get stuffed,' sneered Paul as he counted in the next song.

Exit one arsehole. Old Boys 1—Old Fart 0.

At midnight on New Year's Eve, I was chosen for 'first-footing' duties at home. Here, the youngest at the party stands outside the front door in shirtsleeves and half freezes to death until the horns and buzzers sound twelve o'clock. Then, armed only with a piece of coal (yes, a piece of coal), the harbinger of good fortune is welcomed across the threshold with a drink and a handshake—a reciprocal gesture in exchange for all the good luck he is expected to bring.

I enjoyed my status that night, and still believe to this day that my entrance into 1966 was a deciding influence on England's World Cup victory, the formation of Cream, and the discovery of Jimi Hendrix. Only joking!

Filched Photos and a Fibre-glass Van

A slight, yet pertinent digression. In 1979, as a member of the popular beat combo Whitesnake, I flew to Los Angeles to meet the band's American record company United Artists, attend press meetings, and perform at the UCLA, or the University of California as it's better known. We spent most of our nights at the notorious Rainbow Bar and Grill, a late-night hangout for rock and rollers on Sunset Strip. The Deep Purple half of the band, or the Brass Section, as we'd christened them, had virtually lived in the place during their heyday and introduced the rest of us to some serious nightlife. Which leads me to my original encounter with its namesake—and a far cry from LA's nightlife—the Rainbow Room at Seaton Carew, County Durham.

Situated on the north east coast of England close to Hartlepool, the shabby seaside resort of Seaton Carew was used mainly as a daytime source of entertainment by the local workers and their families, whose hardiness pointed two fingers at the often blustery North Sea. A character named Ken Tyzak ran a promenade cafe which, during the day, offered tea, coffee, ice cream and candy floss, whilst reserving a back room for evening gigs or juke box sessions. The Road Runners made their debut there on the 23rd of January, entertaining a small, yet appreciative audience.

Sitting in that LA establishment over thirteen years later, living the rock and roll dream, my thoughts drifted back to that cold winters night and I thought to myself; "Where did it all go wrong?!"

In the early months of 1966 I was desperate for a new guitar and had my sights set on a Fender Telecaster, a funky-looking instrument with a hard edge favoured by both Eric Clapton and his successor Jeff Beck on their Yardbirds recordings. They were my guitar heroes, as they were to thousands of other young string-benders around the world. Pictures of

Leo Fender's masterpiece adorned my bedroom. My crush would have to endure another three or four months of unrequited passion before I could lay claim to those classic body contours. I knew that my dad would see absolutely no reason to dispense with the Harmony ("A professional guitar"), and reluctantly accepted the fact that absence makes the art grow fonder.

ROAD RUNNERS ITINERARY JAN—FEB '66.
January
1-   *Queens Hotel Hartlepool*
8-   *Queens Hartlepool*
14-   *Langbaurgh Social Club Middlesbrough*
23-   *Rainbow Room Seaton Carew*
24-   *St Pious Church Hall Middlesbrough.*
30-   *Queens Hotel Hartlepool.*

February
7-   *St Pious Church Hall Middlesbrough.*
8-   *Queens Hotel Hartlepool.*
13-   *Queens Hotel Hartlepool.*
14-   *Blackhall Colliery Y.C.*
19-   *Queens Hotel Hartlepool.*
21-   *Rainbow Room Seaton Carew.*
24-   *Billingham Arms Billingham*
25-   *Roseworth Y.C. Stockton.*
27-   *Shildon Workingmen's Club.*

Hardly the best known venues, but at least we didn't have to pay-to-play! By now we were into double figures fee-wise, and the world was at our oyster's feet, or something like that. Nevertheless, I was forced to seek additional employment as a messenger boy for the local newspaper. It was tedious sitting in the corner of a large room attending to the writers and features editors, who all sat round a large table writing articles. When the boredom finally became too much for my inert brain, I would slip out unnoticed to find a dark corridor, where I could gently and repeatedly head-butt the wall.

Necessity being the mother of invention, I eventually came up with a little scam that usually guaranteed a few minutes respite from the indifference of the features department, with the added bonus of obtaining photos of my favourite rock stars, or pop stars as they were called in those days. This little ploy required me to receive a bogus request for a picture of some celebrity or other which could be located in the photo department, a wooden hut on the roof of the building. Once inside, taking care to avoid the suspicious glances of the librarian, I'd strike up a deal with the assistant, a gangly youth with a head-shape not dissimilar to those dried out vegetables you see hanging from the ceilings in Greek restaurants. Intelligence was not his greatest asset.

He'd come up to me, have a quick glance about, and whisper things like, "ey, Mick, them Yardbeds are in!'

Then, for the princely sum of six old pence I could acquire the latest black and white images of my heroes. Because of these surreptitious dealings, photographs of Jeff Beck, Eric Clapton, Steve Winwood et al never appeared in the *Evening Gazette* but on my bedroom wall instead.

As the amount of gigs increased, so did the wear and tear on our old Bedford van. Soon we had no option but to bid farewell to the clapped-out wreck and buy another. Joe announced that he'd found us a Thames fifteen hundredweight van with a lighter, more spacious interior. Well, the chassis and engine were certainly of Thames vintage, as was the upholstery. It was also lighter inside which may have had something to do with the fact that the roof was opaque. Bloody fibreglass! Had we been unfortunate enough to crash into another vehicle, the bodywork would have shattered into a million fragments and bits of us would have been scattered over a wide radius. It was square in shape and though lacking a side hatch, looked rather like one of those mobile shops that haunted council estates in the Sixties. That night, we pulled up outside of Teesside Bridge social club where some comedian asked us for a large sliced loaf and a tin of spam.

A unanimous 'Fuck off!' was the answer.

May 12th saw the Road Runners perform at the cavernous Astoria Ballroom in Middlesbrough. The *Evening Gazette* advertisement described the event as "Teens and Twenties Night", promising "everything you want, we will give you!" Imagine taking that road today. You just wouldn't get away with it. Other irresistible gems on offer included a buffet, discs from eight till twelve and a "snowball", which stood at three pounds. Admission was four shillings, and late transport was available (though not always reliable). An unmissable night!

Around this time, I attempted to gain some much-needed street-cred and took to wearing a pair of small, round-framed dark glasses, as popularised by the Beatles during their *Revolver* period. This groovy look was given the acid test one Sunday afternoon when, in the company of a friend, I attempted to impress the other "groovers" on Redcar prom. My quest for recognition was cruelly cut short by an insensitive café assistant who, when asked for two teas, leaned close to my friend and with a nod in my direction enquired, 'Does 'e take sugar?'

She thought I was blind!

I removed my fashion accessory and glared at her. Ooh, if looks could have killed! The next day I treated myself to 'Telephone Blues' b/w 'I'm Your Witchdoctor' by John Mayall's Bluesbreakers featuring Eric Clapton, which compelled me to bend the strings even more, with or without my dark glasses on.

Back at the *Gazette* office, I ran an errand to the advertising department where I recognised a local bass player called Bruce Thomas. We both nodded in recognition and arranged to meet at lunchtime to discuss music. He was a couple of years older than me, and at eighteen held a good position for his age. It was good to know that there was someone in the building who shared my interest in rhythm and blues, and quite possibly, contraband photos of pop stars. Before I left the room, one of Bruce's colleagues, probably under duress, cursed out loud, which prompted the eldest member of the team to put him in his place.

'The use of obscene language shows a distinct lack of vocabulary. Have some respect for these youngsters.'

'Bollocks!' came the muttered response, resulting in sniggers from the unimpressionable youths.

Immersing ourselves further into rhythm and blues, The Road Runners had now acquired a certain amount of sophistication by including a couple of Booker T. and the M.G.'s tunes in their set. Joe was particularly taken with our rendition of 'Soul Dressing', a cool piece of music that sadly did not require me to employ my recently purchased 'Zonk Tonebender' foot pedal (fourteen guineas worth of instant distortion). The Fuzz Box was well and truly with us, ensuring that rock'n'roll guitarists would never play quietly again. This incited some of us to adopt delicate egos. I recognised my own disposition towards precipitous behaviour after a gig at the Normanby Hotel in nearby Eston, where someone's, no doubt unreasonable comments, left me with no alternative but to announce my early retirement from the band. I sulked in silence until we arrived at my house where I mumbled 'See ya'. The others seemed unimpressed. I remained a victim of injustice for the next couple of days until Joe's tactful cajoling convinced me that I was indeed indispensable (oh dear!). What were the others so guilty of? Who knows?

Meanwhile, Bruce Thomas had teamed up with a couple of local characters whose notoriety had more to do with their personal exploits than musical dexterity. Inspired by early *Melody Maker* reports announcing plans by Eric Clapton, Jack Bruce and Ginger Baker to form Cream, they'd formed a band called The Machine which threatened to set the north east ablaze before invading London. They were rehearsing in a rather questionable part of town at a two-up, two-down belonging to Dave Rea, a local cafe proprietor. As well as providing a rehearsal room, he'd also splashed out on some musical equipment including a rather nice gold-plated Gibson Stereo guitar for the guitarist. Unfortunately, this faith was abused when the band's fingers seemed to be just as adept at taking money from his till as producing sounds from their instruments. He found out and the dream was over, or rather handed over, to the local police department. The Machine never made a record, though the police would eventually award them one each for the illegal usage of a cash register.

Guitar Shuffle

The truth is rarely pure, and never simple—Oscar Wilde.

Back in The Road Runners' camp, Paul Rodgers' voice had matured to such an extent that it was obvious to everybody that he should progress to out-front vocalist, so we urgently needed a bass guitarist. As luck would have it, Bruce had quit The Machine due to 'personality clashes', and we needed to look no further—he was in. The group took on a new lease of life, and inspired by Bruce's hip attitude, started to look like serious contenders for local fame. The Gibson Stereo was apparently up for grabs and I wanted it badly. Without my parents' prior consent, I drew out my entire savings (mostly money left to me by my recently deceased nana) and purchased the instrument from a rather subdued Dave Rea, before sneaking it back home. I knew my dad would never agree to me owning two guitars. I'd become devious and was not proud of it, but such was the lure of a 'real' instrument that my code of ethics temporarily subsided.

So did my commitment, if you could call it that, to my day job. I don't think that my parents were particularly displeased—by now they'd accepted that I would never be Mr nine-to-five, but worse was to come. Shortly after my resignation, the *Evening Gazette* started to print the truth about The Machine, and although Bruce had dropped hints as to the court proceedings, things didn't look too clever in black and white. Our collective parents were not impressed, and for a while Joe was less than supportive. However, the band was sounding good and we carried on like men on a mission.

At some point that summer, Joe managed to record the band's performance during a farmer's ball hosted by Sir William Crossthwaite, at his country home in Great Ayton, a pretty village in North Yorkshire. Due to the fact that the tape machine was only a domestic one-track recorder, the actual sound quality was pretty abysmal. However, it stands as the only documentation of a live Road Runners' show. At one point, Joe picks up the small microphone and to the accompaniment of one of my guitar solos, offers an impromptu commentary:

'This is a great riff by Mike Moody. You'll notice that this boy, although he's only fifteen at this particular time, his jazz improvisations are first class.'

Then, turning to his friend Ron Lampton, another beat group enthusiast, prompts: 'Say something!'

'What, now?' enquires a mike-shy Ron.

'Yes!' affirms Joe.

Ron, accepting his role as 'man on the spot' continued with the rapport. 'Fantastic group! Fantastic, man, fantastic! Great, great, fantastic! Listen, listen, great, great, fantastic! Come on, come on, come on, come on! Fantastic!'

I had the feeling that he was impressed.

On the way home, a fog descended from the depths of nowhere, filling us with a certain amount of concern for our personal safety. As we crawled along at a wary fifteen miles per hour, Ron overtook us in his flashy saloon car at a cool thirty five, blissfully unaware of his position on the wrong side of the dual carriageway.

'Jesus!' yelled Joe, 'he'll have a head-on if he's not careful.'

'He won't get there any quicker, y'know,' opined a voice from the back of the van.

As it turned out, he did.

And he didn't have five drop-off's either.

Inspired by a gig I was lucky enough to experience—John Mayall's Bluesbreakers featuring Eric Clapton (aka God), at the K.D. Club in Billingham—I attacked my new Gibson with a venomous respect, treating myself to a cool black leather jacket in the process. I was feeling as though I'd been reborn, and a serious threat to any local guitarist, when all of a sudden it all started to go horribly wrong. The real owner of the Gibson Stereo turned up at my house and questioned my father about the unpaid monthly instalments on an instrument he'd passed on to Dave Rea long ago. My father hit the bloody roof. The next day he marched me unceremoniously to Rea's café where he demanded back my payment in full. Considering the fact that some rather unpleasant people were hanging around the café at the time, I realise now that my naivety could have resulted in a serious threat to his health. However, his bravery and strength of character demanded that the money be returned to its rightful, albeit stupid owner, and the beloved Gibson was no longer in my possession. I was gutted, and refused to even look at my red Harmony until the next gig. Such was my despondency that I even thought about taking an advanced course in blues at the Teesside College of Further Suffering.

My father eventually forgave me and even agreed to sponsor a hire purchase agreement on a new guitar, part-exchange of course. Under Joe's watchful eye, I did the deal soon after, during a weekend trip to the Windsor Jazz and Blues Festival, an event which caused great excitement in the Road Runners' camp. On that final weekend in July, the country was in a state of near-hysteria due to the World Cup Final at Wembley and my emotional state was heightened even further, by the knowledge that a new instrument could soon be in my clutches.

There is one person knocked down by a car every four minutes in london. He's starting to get really fed up with it—anon.

Joe's Windsor master plan indicated that us Road Runners would travel and sleep in our van, whilst he and Gladys didn't. They'd be in their own car, and would use the site's camping facilities. We headed for London on the Thursday and, as it was our first visit, behaved like excitable teenagers, as indeed we were. Our instructions were to locate Regents Square opposite Kings Cross station (a hooker-free zone in those days) and sleep in our fibreglass chamber until Joe and Gladys arrived. On arrival, we devoured a much-needed cooked breakfast at a local 'greasy spoon', before setting off towards the station to catch a tube to Piccadilly Circus.

'Eh, look, there's one of those Dr Who phone boxes,' observed Dave.

He was right. A big navy blue Tardis just waiting to take us into the future, to a planet far, far away, where the citizens welcomed you with free Fender Telecasters and expensive clothes. Suddenly, the door began to open, causing us to momentarily hold our breaths. Was it the good doctor, or maybe a rogue Dalek bent on mass-extermination? No, just a bobby with acne.

The West End was certainly an eye-opener. I'd never seen so many people, had to dodge so many cars, or been in such close proximity to so many different denominations. We entered naturally into a silly repartee.

'There's Big Ben,' I announced pointing up at the Post Office Tower.

'No it's not,' responded Paul. 'It's Trafalgar Square!'

'Silly buggers!' Joe concluded.

Colin espied a tasty Fender Stratocaster in a nearby music shop and started to drool.

'I'll have one of those one day,' he vowed. And he did.

My own wish to possess a Telecaster was fulfilled at Ivor Mairant's Music Centre, where the legendary guitarist assisted personally in the negotiation. This was the man who'd played with the famous Mantovani Orchestra as well as well as being the author of some highly respected tutors; I was honoured. A part-exchange on the now dreaded red Harmony left me with ninety seven pounds and ten shillings to pay off on hire purchase, an agreement my dad would need to endorse. The deal, with Lloyds & Scottish Finance Ltd of Low Pavement, Nottingham, described the schedule as Fender Telecaster. White. S/No. 104889. 24 Monthly instalments of £4-1s-3d.

As the necessary paperwork would take a couple of weeks to complete, I was allowed ample time in which to count the ensuing days, hours, minutes, seconds and milliseconds until we were re-united. In the meantime, the journey to Windsor made no impression on my memory bank. Totally preoccupied with my own thoughts, the distant and excited voices around me barely registered as we arrived at the festival site early evening.

When people of a certain age revel in Sixties nostalgia, as they often do, you tend to experience the same evocation. Kennedy's death is the obvious, followed by the exploits of the Beatles, the Pill, and England winning the World Cup. Well, the day of the latter I was digging the sounds of the Sixties at Windsor, and received the good news via a singer called Jimmy James, who along with his band the Vagabonds, was cooking up a soul stew on the main stage. There was, of course, a huge response, and even if Jimmy and his dexterous knights of the road had plummeted to the depths of musical absurdity—which they didn't—a standing ovation would still have been academic. It was my first taste of euphoria, and I rather enjoyed it.

The Yardbirds didn't appear, though singer Keith Relf did, to announce that Jeff Beck was ill. Oooh, groans of discontent. Maybe he was suffering from Desert Boot rash. I was not a happy lad. Still, we had Middlesbrough's John McCoy's Crawdaddies who, to Joe's delight, had brought with them crates of Newcastle Brown Ale. A gloriously sunny day, and one that I'll never forget. Ignoring some rather inclement weather, the next day we were treated to the official premier performance of Cream, who were stupendous.

That memorable weekend provided us with the kick-start required to make a serious go of it, and on the way home we talked of nothing else but a move to London. Our fans back in the north east would soon experience a serious change in attitude. A couple of months later, we were lucky enough to see Cream again, at the Kirklevington Country Club shortly after Eric Clapton had lost his legendary Gibson Les Paul to some thieving idiot. I'd brought along a photograph of The Yardbirds (ex-*Evening Gazette* photo naturally), an early shot featuring a young Eric, which I wanted signing. Sensing our excitement, John McCoy showed us to the bands dressing room during the interval, where I nervously thrust the prospective memento into Clapton's hand. He took one look at the photo and burst out laughing.

'It's the mechanical man!' he exclaimed, pointing at the image of rhythm guitarist Chris Dreja.

He seemed to find so much pleasure in sharing this humorous observation with Ginger Baker and Jack Bruce, that I suggested he keep it for future laughs. He thanked me as I gazed enviously at his replacement Les Paul Gold-Top.

'Have a go if you want,' said 'God' as he slipped outside with some nubile thing.

'Ooh, thanks!' I replied excitedly.

'You be careful with that,' ordered an irascible Ginger Baker. 'Seventy bloody quid for this gig. It must 'ave been in the book for months.'

Ten minutes later, Eric returned with a smile on his face. It was clearly good to be God.

Paul was particularly awe-struck by their performance and resolutely declared that his future was in music.

Finsbury Park, Near Scotland

And then the disposessed were drawn west…dusted out, tractored out. Car-loads, caravans, homeless and hungry—John Steinbeck, the Grapes of Wrath.

The buggers couldn't wait to move south, to the smoke. Fantastic! Great!
—Ron Lampton.

The Road Runners continued to run the road to recognition throughout the remainder of 1966, adopting an image of smart but casual individuality. We merged our tailor-made suits into authentic 'gangster-style' outfits, purchased for next to nothing at Stodhard's nearly-new clothes shop, and thought we looked the business. Pin stripes, silk ties, spats, patent leather shoes and even military jackets a la Cream became almost de rigueur. However, a problem arose when Colin, on his way to a sensible future in draftmanship was showing an unwillingness to join the rest of us. In retrospect, this was of course understandable, but completely unacceptable at the time. The rest of us began to isolate him, and Joe obviously felt the vibes. The situation culminated one night at Mr McCoys when the piss-taking got too much for him and he threw the book at us (the accounts were to follow a few days later). He refused to see his younger brother suffer any more and remonstrated in no uncertain terms as to what a complete bunch of so-and-so's we were. He was totally justified in his conclusion that the rest of us were guilty of unkind behaviour, but as a wise man once said, sometimes you've got to be cruel to be kind. So, we were on our own, lacking a mentor, independent and confident in our talent, but oblivious as to the outcome.

Dave, being the eldest and the only driver, assumed responsibility, though Bruce was the obvious choice in dealing with the administrative side. This was to prove to be an unfortunate pairing—the words chalk and cheese being most applicable. Also, they were both ginger-haired, and therefore more prone to unpredictable behaviour (at least, according to the *Viz* book of Gingerists). Disagreements between the pair would usually conclude with a threat of physical abuse by Dave, though Bruce never pushed his luck, subscribing to his theory that "retractions speak louder than turds". Tolerance seemed inevitable.

By now, we'd progressed steadily from R&B into rock-soul, which inspired us to colour our repertoire with versions of such classics as 'Ride Your Pony', 'See-Saw', 'Mustang Sally' and 'Ain't Too Proud To Beg'. I also had the opportunity to put my improvising to the test on 'Green Onions' before the dreaded drum solo gave everyone the chance to either make conversation with the nearest female, or lend an ear to some of the cynics in the audience.

'Sounds like a bloody train crash,' was a popular one, followed closely by 'Oo does 'e think 'e is, Ginger fuckin' Baker?'

These cultured observations were not lost on us and once back on stage, readying ourselves for the conclusive 'Kerrang', we'd pass on these comments to our perspiring percussionist. His response was to reciprocate in his own inimitable style.

'Fuck off yer little bastads, or I'll ploat yer!'

Ah yes, a man all to familiar with the Bard's work. The final flurry on his double bass drum set-up sounded like an amphetamine-crazed mammoth tap dancing on an Anderson shelter. He was, as they say, like a man possessed.

We were exposed to all kinds of characters, but my first experience of a 'chancer' occurred one night when we were booked to appear alongside a band from the Darlington area. There was nothing particularly sinister about that, other than the interest created by the poster, which announced that our opposition would feature "Derek—the blind drummer". Our maturing sense of cynicism, by-passing that human attribute known as humility, looked forward to the ensuing hours with mounting anticipation. We noted that on arrival, Derek was guided immediately to the backstage area, leaving the remainder of the band to transport and set up the equipment. Some minutes later, whilst passing their dressing room, I shot a casual glance. There was Derek, bereft of shades, combing his hair in the mirror. The crafty bastard! Odds-on he owned the van as well.

The Road Runners' onstage behaviour had begun to worry people, and I suppose some of their concern was justified. During one performance at St Patrick's church hall, Paul and myself, by pre-arrangement, enlivened a climactic ending to one of my solos. One of my dad's work socks was doused in lighter fluid, placed on the end of a bamboo cane, then set alight. Paul, acting as the aggressor, then squared up to me in a jousting fashion. Needless to say, the crowd panicked and ended up pressed against the back wall like the intended victims of a firing squad. A priest from the neighbouring church, probably on a goodwill visit to enhance his standing with the youth of the parish, entered at this rather inappropriate moment and thinking the worst, looked heavenwards and crossed himself in prayer. A return booking was never discussed, although I'm sure our perceived mental state was.

Interestingly, Jimi Hendrix adopted an almost identical routine the following year at the Monterey Pop Festival, and though he substituted the bamboo stick and work socks for a guitar, it was plainly obvious where the idea had come from! In fact, we always suspected that both Hendrix and Cream were regularly infiltrating our gigs with spies.

We worked hard on our musical direction and using the influence of Cream, the Paul Butterfield Blues Band and newly discovered Jimi Hendrix as a benchmark, approached our soul-blues covers with renewed inspiration. Paul was coming into his own as a front man, and the band's confidence was growing by the gig.

Meanwhile, Jimmy Page had joined the Yardbirds and in cahoots with Jeff Beck, helped produce the awesome 'Happenings Ten Years Time Ago' and 'Psycho Daisies', landmarks in progressive British rock guitar. Serious stuff. However, we'd gone as far as we could and the big move to London was inevitable. To be quite honest, I couldn't wait. Apart from anything else, my mother was going through some change or other, which wasn't helping family harmony. Perhaps she'd embarked on the Catholic crash diet—lent. I was giving the matter some serious thought prior to a gig, when a girl I'd been seeing, entered the dressing room and sat on my encased Telecaster.

'Gerroff my Telecaster!' I yelled.

'What?' she responded dimly.

'You're sitting on my Telecaster!' I repeated.

'What?' she again responded, in an even dimmer fashion.

Luckily her bum was as soft as her brain and no damage occurred, though her future was guaranteed. Let me out!

Joe eventually forgave us for our decision to oust Colin and would invariably turn up at gigs to lend his support. We were, of course, delighted. Dave had become pretty attached to him and Gladys, spending more time at their house than his own, so he was well made up. We discussed the move to London, and decided that for practical purposes, the van should be converted to accommodate a sleeping area in the form of bunk beds. Practical advice for a four-piece, though not recommended for Welsh choirs. Independence was an important factor in our quest for fame, though sleeping in a fibre glass shell was not necessary going to turn us into overnight sensations. Mind you, at least people would know where to find us.

1966 was a memorable year as musical progression gave serious players the chance to follow their own instincts, without having to behave in such an orderly and predictable fashion. The Beatles were spearheading the transition from pop to rock through albums like *Revolver*. The Yardbirds, Cream and later that year, the Jimi Hendrix Experience all played their part in promoting the electric guitar to its status as the most popular mode of expression for the musical masses. There was talk of a rising suicide rate amongst accordion players and even rumours that Bert Weedon had cultivated an Afro hairstyle. However, to be sixteen in 1966 was like heaven on earth for me and many others.

Once the New Year celebrations had Auld Lang Syne'd themselves into oblivion, we began preparing ourselves for the big move. Bruce busied himself by writing to various agents and selected venues, whilst I turned to Clapton quotes for inspiration:"I have got to the point now where my playing satisfies me technically, and I am now realising the importance of visual impact in the same way Pete Townshend has. I also want to try a few new recording effects and I've got a few ideas for the guitar. I want to get a guitar with two necks. I saw one in an Elvis Presley film poster. It's a guitar with a 12-string neck and a six-string neck on the same body".

I can only assume that Jimmy Page read the same interview.

On the 17th of January, Bruce received a reply from a Mr W.L.Goodman from the head office of Butlins in London, acknowledging "receipt of your letter dated the 11th of January, regarding a summer season engagement for The Road Runners, but regret to inform you that we have no vacancies for this type of group." Looking on the bright side, at least we wouldn't have to go out and buy silly red jackets and greet the mornings with 'Hi-De-hi, Hi-De-Ho' or some other unintelligible gibberish.

At least their main rivals, Pontins, represented by a George E. Coote, promised that "Further consideration will be given to your application early in the New Year and you will be advised accordingly in due course." Whether we were or not is, unfortunately, not recalled, but I can confirm that the band never performed for Fred Pontin's happy bunch. We also received replies from West One Entertainments in London and the Barry Collings Agency in Westcliffe-On-Sea, both of whom expressed interest. Shortly after, on the 17th of February, Bruce handed in his letter of formal notice to the *Evening Gazette*. Two weeks later he became a full-time musician like the rest of us. All we needed now was the full-time work.

Cana Variety Agency was a set-up headed by Jack Fallon, a Canadian who'd been a respected double bassist in his time. We'd noticed their advert in the *Melody Maker* and requested an audition, which they granted, on the 11th of March at the Refectory in Golders Green, North London. This was it boys, we're off! We'd fulfil the remaining local bookings, draw out our savings (mine were pretty meagre) and head off into the sunset, full of optimism and fish paste sandwiches. Bruce had seemingly departed on good terms, as his former employers had granted The Road Runners a little spread in their esteemed organ, publicising the fact that we were leaving "to seek fame and fortune in the cut-throat world of pop". They also informed a no-doubt spellbound readership that Dave would be turning his back on a bright future in welding in order to make his dreams come true.

As we now considered ourselves to be rather cool young men, it suddenly became apparent that our chosen name was no longer in tune with the times. We were aware of the psychedelic culture over in the U.S., and the hip musical trends seemed to be leaning in that direction. So, on Bruce's recommendation we became the Wild Flowers, and were ready to rock. Our respective parents were understandably concerned for our welfare, but drew comfort from the fact that we'd probably be back in a few months. On the 6th of March, our home on wheels was given a once over at the Oxbridge Garage in Stockton, in order to help us "seek fame and fortune in the cut-throat world of pop". Our farewells had that customary teenage awkwardness that left so much unsaid. 'See you, Mam, say goodbye to Dad and Eileen,' was all that I could muster.

My mother smiled, but I think her real feelings remained heartfelt and sorrowful. All that was needed was a chorus from 'It's a long way to Tipperary.' I wasn't alone. The same thing happened at the other three doorsteps, where proud mothers bade farewell to their ambitious sons with egg sandwiches and maternal worry. On Joe Bradley's recommendation, we spent our first night of liberation parked behind a filling station at Apex Corner, a trucker's respite on the outskirts of London. The big adventure had begun and I eventually drifted off into the sleep of the ever-hopeful.

I was roused from my slumbers by the sound of a petrol tanker emptying its contents into the garage forecourt. After a synchronized moan, and due to the lack of any sort of en-suite facilities, we were forced to take a brief hand and face wash in the garage toilet hand basin. No bath, no shower, and no bloody hot water!

We eventually found a welcoming café to ponder our future. Bruce had somehow managed to wangle a gig at the California Ballroom in Dunstable on the night before our audition, supporting American singer Lee Dorsey. He was a particular favourite of ours, and his songs 'Ride Your Pony', 'Workin' in the Coalmine' and 'Holy Cow' had featured in The Road Runners' repertoire. Although a little apprehensive towards playing to a southern audience, deep down we were all pretty excited as to the outcome. Being neither paid off nor attacked, we were off to a reasonable start, fortified by the goodwill shown to us by Dorsey's backing group, a bunch of Glaswegians called The Scots of St. James. Amidst the usual volleys of good-humoured banter, there seemed to be the suggestion that an attic flat was available in the madhouse they shared with another bunch of Jocks in Finsbury Park, London N.4.

'Hey, youse lot wannae crash sumwhere? Come tae our gaff, y'ill nae regret it.'

That night we 'crashed' at a local bed and breakfast hotel, and awoke refreshed in the knowledge that so far we hadn't 'regretted it'.

It proved to be an eventful weekend. We journeyed to Finsbury Park to inspect the attic flat, but when the landlord—an Irishman with huge hands—showed us into the garret, we immediately began to 'regret it'. Actually, it wasn't too bad. It had four beds, a single-ring gas appliance, a small gas fire, wardrobe, chairs and en-suite sink. Obviously, there wasn't much room to swing the proverbial.

'Wher'm a gonna set me drums up?' asked Dave, eyeing the tiny island of space in the middle of the room. We looked at each other in disbelief.

He set them up the next day, then warned, 'Don't anybody sneeze near them—it'll rust the chrome.'

The trouble was that anywhere in the room was near the newly-assembled double drum kit. It was no good, they'd have to go. The next day Dave dismantled his kit, we paid a week's rent in advance (seven pounds), then set out for the audition.

The gig at the Refectory was an apparent success, as Cana Variety Agency invited us to their office first thing Monday afternoon to sign a four-and-a-half year sole agreement, for a commission of ten percent. However, an extra five percent would be commissioned on all weekly earnings over one hundred and fifty pounds, and yet another five percent on earnings exceeding two hundred. This particular stipulation was to remain unfulfilled. Clause 7 stated "that if during the probationary period (twenty six weeks) the agent shall fail to procure for the Artiste engagements producing an amount of 1,300 pounds then this agreement shall ipso facto be deemed to be cancelled". Considering that thirteen hundred pounds was a substantial amount of money in 1967 and our earning capacity per engagement in March that year was twelve pounds, there was every possibility that we'd be free agents by September, unless Cana secured us 4.15 gigs a week from that moment on. By April we were a twenty pounds a night attraction, but their options on our contract still seemed an unlikely prospect.

Due to our tender age, Paul, Bruce and myself were required by law to seek written permission from our parents, in order to validate our contract with Cana. Although we foresaw no real problems, a letter from Jack Fallon informing us that a tour of Scotland had been arranged did lend some weight to the subject. The Wild Flowers were to perform at six venues in nine days at halls in the extreme north of Scotland, a prospect that filled us with such excitement that we couldn't wait to tell the Scottish lads downstairs. Actually, they were next door too; three bands in all, including the Senate, a soul band that often accompanied visiting American singers. Their line-up featured the late Robbie McIntosh of the Average White Band, and singer-guitarist Alex Ligertwood, who eventually joined Santana. Then of course, there was the Scots of St. James, plus the Fancy Bred. The latter included Alan Gorrie in their line-up. He soon joined the Scots of St. James before teaming up with McIntosh in the Average White Band. Phew! Still with me?

Prior to our trek into the unknown wilds of Scotland, we had three engagements to honour. One was more dishonourable—well, as far as Dave was concerned. The Black Dog pub in Southwark was hardly a prestigious venue, but it was a gig and we needed it. For some reason, Dave got pissed and was unable to perform the second set. The only solution was for singer and guitarist to become instant multi-instrumentalists—me on drums and Paul on guitar. The landlord was not impressed and refused to pay us. Who could blame him? Being a big bugger, we weren't going to argue the toss. Afterwards, we sat in the van until Dave was sober enough to drive us home. Scotland here we come.

We planned to break up the mammoth journey by stopping off at our respective homes for a night, grabbing a good night's sleep after first presenting our worried parents with the opportunity to monitor our gradual weight loss. A huge home-made dinner followed by pudding was devoured to "help us put that weight back on".

We arrived in Elgin, tired and slightly disorientated. Dave, as the only driver, looked as though he'd been interrogated—mad staring eyes, drained features and shaking hands. Mind you, that was pretty much how he looked anyway.

'Friggin''ell—am knackered!' he admitted.

'I know,' I replied blandly as I watched my breath condense in the dank atmosphere.

An eerie silence surrounded us, a ghostly air that cast a defiant V-sign at the Swinging Sixties from the opposite end of the A1. Suddenly, Stockton seemed attractive. For those with limited geographical knowledge, Elgin is of a similar longitude to Stavanger in Norway. That is to say, rather north. We were to head for Myrtle Cottage, Lossie Wynd, the property of a Mrs Macbean, which would be our home for the next nine days.

Our host was a plump, genial soul whose guest book bore witness to names famous and not so famous, who'd slept under her roof. 'Aye, here's the Beatles,' she indicated proudly. 'Nice laddies. Cheeky wee scamps!' I'd never heard them described quite that way before, but she seemed rather maternal in her affections. Then she made it clear as to her expectations. 'Nae gerils in the rooms at anytime, day or night and brakefast at nine.'

Breakfast at nine? We were teenagers for God's sake—we slept a lot!

'Eight early mornings' I kept repeating, until I drifted off into a deep slumber.

'Brakefast, com'n boys, it's ten tae nine an' the porridge is gonnae ge' cold.'

'Eh? Wha'? Who?' was the best I could manage as my body went into shock.

She flung back the curtains with the kind of gusto normally associated with Hattie Jaques or Joan Simms in the *Carry On* films. Muttered obscenities could be heard in the next room. As we were the only residents, I assumed it was another unimpressed Wild Flower.

'*!*!*!*!' groaned Bruce.

'*!*!*!* *!*!' agreed Dave.

'*!**!*!**' hissed Paul.

'*!*!!* *!**!' cursed yours truly.

Mrs Mac, her mission accomplished, headed back downstairs, la-la-ing a jolly little tune. 'Help yoursel' t' thae jam. Porridge'll be ready in a wee minute,' she trilled.

Oh, no! I was back at bloody Hexham Summer Camp! Somebody suggested dumping generous amounts of jam into the gruel. It turned out to be a wise suggestion. The toast was acceptable, with lots of jam of course. And by the time the fry-up came, we were digging in heartily. Well, for a pound a night, with a sandwich supper thrown in, I don't suppose it was a bad deal. We'd sometimes show our appreciation by squeezing out an early morning trouser cough, though we were courteous enough to wait until La Macbean was back in her kitchen. I'm sure she'd heard it all before.

Our itinerary dictated that we worked three consecutive days, didn't work for three consecutive days, then worked the remaining three consecutive days. I think the agent must have been Norwegian, because it's very similar to the schedule worked over there. Maybe he also owned all the shops in and around Elgin. After becoming bored shitless by our second day off, we resorted to spending the pittance he paid us on useless goods, just to relieve the monotony. I bought a cut-price Joe Brown LP on the Music For Pleasure label and a pair of green underpants. You can draw your own conclusions.

By the third day off, the boredom was so severe that a tour of the ruins of a rain-swept Elgin Abbey seemed in order. We should have gone the whole hog and visited Culloden Moor, just to cheer ourselves up.

The gigs were odd, but the audiences probably thought the same about us. We weren't exactly the Rockin' Berries, and the response was pretty uninspiring. The stage at Elgin Town Hall was up in the balcony, which gave people a fine view of our heads. Those that bothered to watch our set must have returned home with severe neckache. Then there was the clientele at the Beach Ballroom in Aberdeen who spent the whole evening strolling round the dance floor in a huge circle, seemingly oblivious to the efforts of the bands on stage. Very strange.

In a place called Buckie, I was studying a poster advertising the forthcoming May Queen competition, when a couple of local lads walked past. Noting my apparent interest, one of them turned to me and said:

'I hope it's more successful than last year.'

'Why, what happened? I enquired.

'Nobody won!' He replied, then burst out laughing.

Though we all had a wee chortle, I knew I'd be happy to get back in my mobile bunk bed and head southwards.

We repeated our upward journey plan and stopped off to stay with our families on the return journey, regaling them with tales of boredom and early mornings in the Caledonian wilderness. I visited Hamilton's music shop and cheered myself up by part-exchanging my trusty but somewhat underpowered Gibson Varitone amplifier for a Marshall 50 watt set-up, which included a rather large 4x12 speaker cabinet. We set off soon after, with mam-made lunches, to sort this 'London lot' out.

Doom and Gloom in N.4.

In our estimation, the agency was failing on their part by not supplying enough work to enable us to regard ourselves as professional musicians. In their defence, they cited the fact that bookings had to be made months in advance and that we were relative newcomers. Fine, but we just wanted to get out of the attic. They did manage to secure one quick booking, at a dingy club in Edmonton, north London where the owner turned up late and virtually ignored us. His unwelcoming manner may have been influenced by the poor advance ticket sales—the venue was so poorly attended that when we hit the stage it made Hades look lively. And the audience was so small and unresponsive, when they stood in a line it looked like Mount Rushmore.

The food parcels and money from home helped. One of my mother's letters expressed her concern for my well-being.

'Hope the fishcakes I sent in the parcel were fresh when they got to you. I was a bit worried because sometimes the parcels get delayed and you don't always get them delivered until a few days later. I will be enclosing a ten shilling note for the duffle coat of yours which your dad sold to one of his workmates (hope he did the right thing).'

He was still at it! Mind you, it was appreciated and would eventually pay for my kaftan.

April's *Beat Instrumental* informed us that the Yardbirds would be using tapes on stage to help reduce those awkward moments encountered during guitar changes. The idea, attributed to Jimmy Page, included snippets of well known tunes such as 'Batman' to allow him time to change from ordinary guitar to six-string bass, sitar, 12-string guitar or an ordinary bass. Suddenly, and for no apparent reason, I felt my first pangs of homesickness. Finsbury Park on a wet, dark night could dampen the hardest of hearts. Without even a television to turn to for distraction, I lay on my bed and listened to the rain, imagining cooking smells back home. My mother had always maintained that food was an important part of a balanced diet. She was right; I didn't have any and was starting to feel decidedly unbalanced.

A little devil appeared in my head, its face contorted into a wicked leer. It tormented me with unattainable pleasures: 'Steak and kidney pie; jam roly-poly and custard!' Aaagh! I picked up the *Beat Instrumental* and continued where I'd left off. Under the headline, 'The Sounds I Like' by Britain's top guitarists, one found out that Jeff Beck liked a "good chunky rhythm sound which can be turned into a powerful whining lead sound when required". Tony Hicks from the Hollies, on the other hand, whilst agreeing with Beck over the "good, thick, chunky sound", admitted that he'd "never really gone for all this whining guitar stuff". Fair enough, though I bet at that particular moment they were both tucking into home-made cottage pie and chips. Bastards! The record player blasted out 'A Hard Road' by John Mayall and the Bluesbreakers, who were, in all probability, both working and eating that night. Was there no justice in the world?

Somewhere in Chicago, the down-hearted blues singer was probably still better off than me.

Twenty five years in the business. Five years playing and twenty years hanging about—Charlie Watts.

This 'resting between engagements' was proving to be counter-productive. When pretentious types prattle on these days about male bonding, I find it difficult to keep a straight face. If you're stuck in a room suitable for one, with three others and a drum kit day and night, you soon get to know each other, warts an' all. It's true to say that ignorance can be blissful and youthful enthusiasm has its merits, but this kind of undisciplined billeting is strictly for the dedicated.

However, distraction occurred in the form of two girls from Hartlepool, who provided Paul and I with the best sort of distraction, though my distinct lack of experience made it hard going, if you'll excuse the pun. It was hardly romantic, considering Dave and Bruce were in the same room 'sleeping', but welcome nevertheless. On the fifteenth of May, I wrote a letter home and in a short, albeit enthusiastic correspondence, informed my family about the previous nights gig at Blaises club in Kensington—"the posh part of London". Celebrities including Susan Hampshire were in evidence, and it seems that a girl who worked for Cat Stevens' producer Mike Hurst approached me at the interval. She suggested that we call him regarding a record test, and in all likelihood, we did. Obviously nothing came of it.

The music press heralded shock news. Jeff Beck had left the Yardbirds during an American tour, citing work pressure and internal friction as the main causes. Back at his London flat, he remarked that he was "eating things like yoghurt and downing a lot of vegetables". Aha! So that was the secret to his virtuoso performances—a controlled diet! Within minutes, I was scouring the nearest supermarket for my winning formula. Though the yoghurts were easily secured, the choice of vegetables posed a problem. Beck's quote made no mention of a meat accompaniment, so, bearing this in mind, I chose two that were the most appealing to my taste buds—sprouts and a medium sized Swede. Up until that moment I'd never actually cooked a vegetable as my mother had always been there to attend to such chores. And anyway cooking at the flat was always kept to a minimum. I deduced that by boiling them together in the same pan, the end result should be satisfactory. Alas, the feast was hardly fit for a king, let alone a prince. Or even Prince the dog. It looked and tasted like a chemistry experiment. Thankfully the strawberry yoghurt helped to take away most of the taste. Jeff Beck was welcome to his own style, thank you very much. I'd persevere with my own, heavily influenced by steak pies, chips and Shreddies.

The next day we made our way to the famous Marquee Club where John Mayall's Bluesbreakers were appearing. We were desperate to catch their set as the band, featuring Peter Green, was legendary to us young and impressionable ones. Of course, we had no money to buy a ticket, so we hung around backstage and offered to help Mayall's roadie with the equipment, using our cunning to avoid detection. It worked! Peter Green was spellbinding, and the support group Family wore candy-striped suits and performed a version of the Muddy Waters' classic 'Rollin' Stone'. During the gig we all shared a coke, then went home on the bus.

Before the month was out, I was the proud owner of another guitar, or should I say another Fender Telecaster, acquired from Larry Macari's Musical Exchange in Charing Cross Road. They agreed to take mine, plus twenty quid (which I blagged from my dad). It helped bolster my sagging self-esteem.

Cheer up! The worst is yet to come!—Philander Chase Johnson.

Disaster struck on June 3rd when the van's big ends went en route to Great Yarmouth. It groaned and came to a halt on the A12, along with Dave's determination to make a name for himself "in the cut-throat world of pop". We were well and truly stuffed. All we could do was regroup and hopefully get the van towed back to Finsbury Park. Bruce and myself took it upon ourselves to hitchhike back and acquire the services of one Edmund McGonagle—our landlord's Man Friday—to save the day. He always liked our van. 'Sure, dat's a fine lukin' t'ing,' he'd often remarked.

By the time we finally arrived at the flat, we were tired, cold, and laden with first-hand knowledge of what it's really like to have the blues. Somewhere, on a dark lay-by in Essex, Dave and Paul were, no doubt, bonding, whilst a blues singer in Chicago was drinking our health.

Edmund agreed to help us—at a price. He'd tow the crippled vehicle back, then claim it as his own, with an offer to 'help us out' on future dates. We had little choice but to accept. When he returned later that night, only Paul emerged.

'Where's Dave?' I enquired.

'He's buggered off home,' retorted an unimpressed Paul. 'He rang his dad and he came and took him back.' He looked really pissed off.

'Good riddance,' declared Bruce, now hopefully free from the wrath of Dave.

We softened our acute despondency with a cup of tea and a biscuit, and agreed to soldier on. On the subject of soldiers, Dave's father was an ex-Major in the British army who, appreciating our pioneering spirit, had given us his blessing prior to our move to London. According to Paul, he was less than impressed with Dave's lack of stiff upper lip in overcoming our little mishap, and had delivered some serious admonishment before taking him home. Later, he offered the rest of us his good wishes, expressing an admiration of our loyalty—an attribute seemingly lacking in his own offspring. We all agreed that he was a prat for dropping us in it.

'The youth of today—put 'im in the bloody army!' I joked. It was not appreciated.

Desperation set in. Not only did we have no money, we had no drummer, no van, and hardly any gigs in the book. To perpetuate our existence

Above: Middlesbrough, 1960. Street football team, Micky Moody far left. *(Micky Moody)*

Right: Micky Moody at St. Thomas' school, 1963. *(Micky Moody)*

Below: St Thomas' school team, 1963, Micky Moody far right. *(Micky Moody)*

NATURAL mood and backcloth. PAL PICTURES, Middlesbrough.

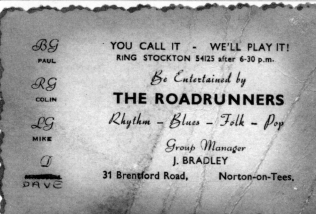

BG
PAUL

RG
COLIN

LG
MIKE

D
DAVE

YOU CALL IT - WE'LL PLAY IT!

RING STOCKTON 54125 after 6-30 p.m.

Be Entertained by

THE ROADRUNNERS

Rhythm — Blues — Folk — Pop

Group Manager

J. BRADLEY

31 Brentford Road,   Norton-on-Tees.

Above: The Road Runners, 1965. (L-R) Dave Usher, Colin Bradley, Paul Rodgers, Micky Moody. *(Micky Moody)*

Left: "You call it, we'll play it!" Publicity card announces The Road Runners, managed by Joe Bradley.

Below: The Road Runners first official photoshoot in Joe Bradley's back garden in 1965. *(Micky Moody)*

Opposite: Road Runners publicity shots, 1965

ROAD......
RUNNERS

ROCK &
SOUL :
GROUP

Top left: Colin Bradley & Micky Moody, Joe Bradley sitting, 1965. *Micky Moody*

Middle left: John McCoy's prophetic *Evening Gazette* review, 1966: "Paul Rodgers has an amazing voice and will undoubtedly emerge as one of the greatest rock singers in the world."

Bottom left: Road Runners, Black Hall Colliery, Co Durham, 1965. *Micky Moody*

Above: Joe Bradley with early roadies Dave & Ritchie at the bar. *Micky Moody*

Right: Wild Flower Moody shows off new haircut and Telecaster, Finsbury Park, London, 1967. *Micky Moody*

Below: A psychedelic Wild Flowers, Golders Hill Park, London, 1967. (L-R) Andy Borenious, Bruce Thomas, Paul Rodgers, Micky Moody. *Micky Moody*

Thur. 1st
THE BEATSTALKERS
The Groop

Fri. 2nd
Blues Night:
SAVOY BROWN BLUES BAND
Gordon Smith

Sat. 3rd
NEAT CHANGE
and Supporting Group

Mon. 5th
THE NITE PEOPLE
Yes!

Tue. 6th
THE CRAZY WORLD
OF ARTHUR BROWN
East of Eden
(Members' Tickets 7/6 available in advance from
July 30th. Non-members 10/- on evening).

Wed. 7th
SPOOKY TOOTH
Clouds

Thur. 8th
THE NICE
The Glass Menagerie
(Members 7/6. Non-members 10/-)

Fri. 9th
Blues Night:
JETHRO TULL
Black Cat Bones

Sat. 10th
NEAT CHANGE
The Boots

Mon. 12th
Blues Night:
THE TASTE
Keef Hartley

Tue. 13th
JOHN MAYALL'S
BLUESBREAKERS
Duster Bennett
(Members' Tickets 7/6 available in advance from
Aug. 6th. Non-Members 10/- on evening)

Wed. 14th
The Fantastic
JOE COCKER
The Groop

Thur. 15th
THE BEATSTALKERS
The Open Mind

Fri. 16th
Blues Night:
TEN YEARS AFTER
Tramline

Sat. 17th
NEAT CHANGE
Yes!

Mon. 19th
THE NITE PEOPLE
The Cortinas

Tue. 20th
TONY RIVERS and the CASTAWAYS
The Glass Menagerie
(Members' Tickets 7/- available in advance from
Aug. 13th. Non-members 8/6 on evening)

Wed. 21st
The Fantastic
JOE COCKER
The Open Mind

Thur. 22nd
THE NICE
East of Eden
(Members 7/6. Non-Members 10/-)

Fri. 23rd
Blues Night:
JETHRO TULL
Duster Bennett

Sat. 24th
NEAT CHANGE
Young Blood

Mon. 26th
Blues Night:
THE TASTE
Tramline

Tue. 27th
MARMALADE
The Gun
(Members' Tickets 7/6 available in advance
from Aug 20th. Non-Members 10/- on evening).

Wed. 28th
The Fantastic
JOE COCKER
Clouds

Thur. 29th
THE BEATSTALKERS
The Dream Police

Fri. 30th
Blues Night:
TEN YEARS AFTER
Keef Hartley

Sat. 31st
NEAT CHANGE
The Open Mind

EVERY SUNDAY
"WHOLE LOTTA SOUL"
featuring
RADIO ONE DJ STUART HENRY
and the best in recorded "Soul music"
also live groups
Members : 5/-   Guests : 7/6

All Programmes are subject to alteration and the Management cannot be held responsible
for non appearance of artistes.

Printed by Richard Moore & Leslie Ltd. 57 Poland Street, W.1.
Published by Marquee Publicity Ltd., 18 Carlisle St., W.1

Left: 16th & 26th August 1968, Tramline
support Ten Years After and Taste
at London's illustrious Marquee Club
amongst the pick of the talent of '67.

Above: Micky Moody and Terry
Sidgewick, 1968. *Micky Moody*

Below: Tramline. (L-R) Terry Sidgewick,
Micky Moody, Terry Popple, John McCoy.
Micky Moody

Above: Tramline at a Middlesbrough boutique, 1968. *Micky Moody*

Right and bottom: Micky Moody on tour with The Mike Cotton Sound backing former Manfred Mann singer, Paul Jones in Sweden, 1969. *Micky Moody*

Below: *Somewhere Down the Line*, the first Tramline album.

TONIGHT'S PROGRAMME

Programme subject to alteration at the management's discretion

*Joe Cocker & the Grease Band will not appear at the Birmingham and Lincoln concerts

1 Lucas & the Mike Cotton Sound

2 Mike Quinn

3 The Iveys

4 Mike Quinn

*5 Joe Cocker & the Grease Band

INTERVAL

In accordance with the requirements of the local authority: 1. All gangways, passages and staircases must be kept entirely free from chairs or any other obstruction. 2. The public shall be permitted to leave by all exit and entrance doors - for each performance of entertainment. 3. No smoking shall be permitted to take place on the stage except as part of a performance or entertainment. 4. The safety curtain must be lowered and raised at least once during every performance or entertainment, to ensure its being kept in proper working order.

6 Lucas & the Mike Cotton Sound

7 Mike Quinn

8 The Marmalade

9 Mike Quinn

10 Gene Pitney

MOVES OF VEGETABLE CENTURIES

Above left: Programme for the Gene Pitney tour, with Mike Cotton Sound as backing band.
Micky Moody

Above: Probably the strangest album title of all time, Tramline's 1968 second album *Moves of Vegetable Centuries*.

Left: Micky Moody in Germany recently, playing alongside former Family frontman Roger Chapman.
Jo and Anja Sudau

Below: Zoot Money's bizarre surrealist eponymous album cover, 1970.

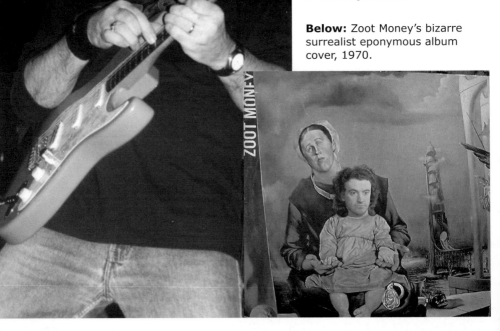

we took to selling our stage clothes to the Scottish lads downstairs, and existed on cereal and pancakes, plus the odd yoghurt filched from the local grocery store. Some days we'd just eat what was there; maybe an Eccles cake, or a tin of peas on toast. My 28-inch waist jeans started to sag, as did my enthusiasm. Suddenly, I felt very homesick. Lying on my bed, alone in that attic flat listening to Ray Davies singing 'Waterloo Sunset' on the tiny transistor radio, I experienced a new kind of emotion—melancholia. There was only one answer. We'd have to take on some kind of supplementary work.

It was a daunting prospect. The local employment office offered us a three-day a week job making aluminium deck chairs at the Good Value Furniture factory in Islington. We accepted it—or should I say Paul and myself accepted it. Bruce, under the delusion that he was a 'professional' musician, refused to be associated with losers and stayed in bed, rising only to check the post for money from home. The three-day week turned out to be just that. I worked the three days and retired the same week, citing repetitive deckchair-making fatigue as an excuse.

So, more clothes were sold to Scotsmen with regular employment, by now including Onnie McIntyre, yet another future Average White member. Legendary roadie 'Buby' Daniels had also swelled their ranks. I was left with one old coat, one pair of jeans, one pair of trousers, two shirts, a T-shirt, two pairs of shoes and some ragged underwear. If things had gotten any worse, I'd have died of exposure. I tried to keep my spirits up by remembering a quote Jeff Beck had made about his financial state after leaving the Yardbirds.

"At the moment I'm wearing a pair of Levis and a five bob T-shirt. If finances improve I'll own two pairs of Levis and two T-shirts".

Thankfully, Edmund MaGonagle kept his side of the bargain and got the van back on the road, promising to honour his promise to 'help us out'. We hoped that we didn't have to undertake another Scottish tour. His day job would put the mockers on that.

Our quest for a replacement drummer was momentarily relieved by hiring a 'dep' for an impending gig at the Morris School of Hairdressing in Great Windmill Street, W.1. He was too old to be considered as a replacement, and he chain-smoked, though once he did stop during the set to snort some snuff. After we paid him for the gig he went straight to the nearest shop and spent it on cigarettes. Ironically, the next guy we tried was named Dave; we ascertained this after answering his advert in *Melody Maker*. He wasn't a bad player, but he seemed to be more concerned with aesthetics than music and we passed on him. The band's direction was still leaning towards a Rock-Tamla-Hendrix-Blues mould, with Jeff Beck's newly formed group featuring Rod Stewart acting as a benchmark for inspiration. All we needed now was a drummer who felt the same way. Alternatively, three stunning-looking nymphomaniac millionairesses would have relieved the situation. The bitches never materialised. They'll just never know what they missed.

London's West End always provided an attractive alternative to rainy afternoons in Finsbury Park. It was still a swinging place, with plenty of beautiful people and groovy sights. Dobell's jazz and blues record shop in Charring Cross Road was a great place to browse. I put any spare cash I had in an old Oxo tin and then head 'up west' to buy Django Reinhardt, Robert Johnson, Wes Mongomery and Lonnie Johnson, and vow to get a nice steel string acoustic when we'd cracked it. For guitar strings I'd head for Selmers, one of the country's most established shops. Here, the three of us would often chat to a young assistant called Paul Kossoff, whose father David was the comedy actor and star of TV and films. It transpired that Paul's friend and neighbour up in Golders Green was a drummer looking for a band and had a good feel for blues. Could this be our man? So we hung around until Paul clocked off, then headed for the bus stop where we boarded a welcoming Routemaster and headed for the upstairs smoking deck (yes, SMOKING). He offered me a Piccadilly tipped and I accepted, before breaking into casual conversation.

'What guitar do you play.'

'Maple neck Tele, what about you?'

'Oh, a '59 Les Paul.'

'What, like Clapton's on The Bluesbreakers album?'

'Er, yea.'

The lucky sod. I was, to say the least, extremely envious.

New Drummer, New Teeth, New Start

Golders Green was a prosperous area of north London, known more for its large Jewish community than blues-rock drummers of Swedish-Russian descent. Andy Borenious had neither the classic look of Russian nor Swede, he was kind of in the middle—with glasses. Paul Kossoff made the initial introductions and we entered into the sort of middle class household that was light years away from my own cloth cap origins. Mrs Borenious, an earth mother, made us feel at home and fed us with pasta and lentils before predicting a secure future with her young Andy at the helm. After three months or so of attic dwelling, it sure felt good. If Andy's drumming was as convincing as his mother's optimism, we'd do no wrong in following her advice. Mr Borenious smiled; so did we.

Q: How do you stop three teenagers from smiling?

A: You take them to an attic flat in Finsbury Park via a long bus journey.

Back at the garret, the gloomy atmosphere of our bare sixty watt bulb was in danger of obliterating our recent encounter, so we switched the bloody thing off and retired to our beds.

The 'Summer of Love' of 1967 brought changes both in lifestyles and clothes' sense. As we were severely lacking on both counts, a change was as good as a rest. We wandered the streets of London's West End, soaking up the atmosphere. Shops with names such as Kaleidoscope and Granny Takes a Trip were selling kaftans, beads, crushed velvet trousers and hashish-smoking paraphernalia. I assumed that joss sticks were drugs and avoided them at all costs, believing them to be made from 'pep' pills and hemp, a combination that would eventually send you crazy. Well, as Howlin' Wolf sang: "I'm just a poor boy, I'm a long ways from home". And I was.

Drugs never entered into our little world because we weren't offered any, and if we had been, we wouldn't have had the money to pay for them. In retrospect, I don't think that we'd have dabbled anyway. Mind-expansion was for 'older' people as far as I was concerned, and we existed purely for our music. It would be a while before I'd succumb to darker temptations.

Andy's initiation as a working Wild Flower took place on Saturday June 24th, at the Bedford College of Education, Bedford, Bedfordshire (where else?). Edmond McGonagle turned up freshly scrubbed, suited and booted and accompanied by his other half, who wore a frock and a cardigan. We wore what we hadn't sold to the Jocks, which wasn't a lot. It must have been an odd sight; the scruffy young bluesers and the Jim Reeves fan club, sharing a pleasant summer's afternoon drive in a re-cycled bread van.

'Will yez be playin' anyt'ing we noze?' asked Mrs Edmond, clutching her copy of the Catholic Herald. Edmond, who'd heard us rehearsing in the flat, smiled knowingly.

A few days later, I woke up early with a painful toothache. Having suffered at the hands of an insensitive dentist some years previously, I tried to reassure myself that the pain would recede. By the third day, my face was so swollen I was sucking soup through a straw. It was no use. I'd have to visit the nearest dentist.

Dilip Chowdhury (LDS RCS) was, as his name suggests, of Asian descent. He possessed that gentle vocal lilt characterised so often by Peter Sellers, which helped reduce my acute fear. He took one look into my swollen orifice and announced: 'You have not been to the dentists for eight years.' He was absolutely right. How did he know? Maybe in India they read teeth instead of palms.

A LIMITED CONVERSATION IN A DENTIST'S CHAIR.
'Open wide. Ah, when did you break your two front teeth?'
'Aaeurrgh ag arre gorr orh.'
'After I've finished with your fillings, I'd like to repair them, OK?'
'Aarr, ourr agga aer ohrr oah.'

Due to my painful condition, the treatment would begin within a couple of days. I went home for more soup.

My dental arches must have had more cavities than the walls in an average Sixties council flat, because it required three visits to repair years of sugar abuse and disregard for toothbrushes. Then it was on to the real issue—cosmetic surgery. My two front teeth were a disaster. Due to an impromptu attempt at trying to take a bite out of the pavement some seven years earlier, they'd remained in a jagged state ever since. Now it was time to return them to their former glory—or so I thought. He experimented with the remains of my original teeth and fitted 'temporaries', a brace of off-white abominations that Ken Dodd would have shook his head in disbelief at. Later on that day, as I was trying to decide what to eat, Bruce offered me a lump of wood to gnaw on. Ha, bloody ha. It got worse. Once the 'temps' were removed, the fun really started. By melding gold and various pieces of coloured enamel, Mr Chowdhury (LDS RCS) created a spectacle rarely seen before on a sixteen-year-old boy. When I smiled, I gave the impression that I was trying to swallow a pair of cuff-links. West Indians would stop me in the street to marvel at Dilip's handiwork, occasionally lifting my top lip for a closer inspection. This situation prevailed in my mouth for another four years, until a sympathetic dentist in Shepherds Bush transformed Dilip's creation back to something resembling, well, human teeth.

A much welcomed period of light relief was provided, albeit unknowingly, by a certain Mr H.G. Lonsdale, native of north Yorkshire. The poor man in question had approached us the previous summer after a gig in Brotton, with the sole purpose of impressing us with his lyrical efforts. After a brief chat he departed, leaving a couple of examples of his 'work' for our perusal. Needless to say, the journey home was interrupted by fits of laughter and youthful disbelief. Was he serious? One of his observational masterpieces paid homage to a small passenger vehicle manufactured by the Meschershmitt Company.

I saw a bubble car scream down the road last night,
Painted pretty colours, red blue and white...etc

I honestly can't remember the remaining twenty-four verses which is probably a blessing, but they certainly don't write them like that any more. In fact, they didn't even write them like that then. Twelve months on, having endured disappointment, upheaval and dental pain, I suggested to Paul and Bruce that a degree of levity could be achieved courtesy of the Bard of Brotton. Keeping his address was a masterstroke; we wrote him a letter and retired amid a glow of mischievous anticipation.

Our act of wickedness was based entirely on The Monkees and their successful TV show, where the co-habiting pop group had fun and adventures on their way to the top. If they could do it, why couldn't The Wild Flowers? We wrote to H.G. explaining our intentions, stressing that the television company involved had insisted that we change our name immediately to the Sausage and Mash. Within a few days we had our treasured reply, which included the freshly written 'Sausage and Mash' theme tune. Unfortunately, I'm not in possession of a copy of the classic work, though the opening lines will remain forever etched in my mind:

> If you hear a sudden crash or a supersonic boom,
> It's that group, sausage and mash, flyin' across the room.

Unaware of our piss-taking, he wrote a few more times in the vain hope of receiving some kind of news regarding the proposed Sausage and Mash TV Show. He never got a reply.

After scraping enough money together, the four of us lashed out on some cool kaftans, whilst quickly coming to the conclusion that The Wild Flowers was uncool. We became The Wildflowers. Yeah, cool or what?

After a few more gigs, the novelty of a new name wore off for Edmund and we were once more vanless. We didn't even bother to argue about the rights to the vehicle, as none of us could drive. A few days later we decided to move closer to Andy's neck of the woods, taking up residence at 102 Sumatra Road, West Hampstead, another bedsit with three beds. As the room boasted a couple of chairs and a small table, we didn't actually need to sit on the beds. Bloody luxury! Relaxing in more formal positions, we studied our imminent workload. It was not particularly encouraging.

WILDFLOWERS ITINERARY JULY—'67.
1-Castle Club, RAF Conningsby, Lincs.
2-Witchdoctor Club, St Leonards.
7-Tarpots Club, Benfleet.
8-007 Club, Woodford.
11-London College of Fashion.
14-Tarpots Club, Benfleet.
15-Orford Cellar Club, Norwich.
21-Royal Clarendon Hotel, Gravesend. (eventually cancelled).

There's every possibility that the cancelled gig in Gravesend was due to transportation problems, as we had to hire a 'man with a van' to get us to the venues. I seem to remember a guy called Bob coming to the rescue most of the time in his trusty Commer. It worked well until Mrs Borenious, in a moment of madness, unjustifiably accused the poor man of being some sort of fifth-columnist and a bad influence on her boys. He was obviously upset, but we managed to convince him of his indispensability, thus securing a much-needed gig, as well as a change of scenery. Nevertheless, he was not impressed.

Judging by the itinerary, we seemed to be popular at Tarpots Club in Benfleet, and presumably I chatted up an admirer, as I received a letter from a Barbara Clark of Basildon. She informed me that she was seventeen years old (I always had a soft spot for the older woman), was born in West Ham, and moved to Basildon when she was two. She then went on to tell me that she worked in Fleet Street as an invoice typist, and oh, did I work, and what did I do in my spare time? Did I like Tamla Motown, mod bands, soul music and Cat Stevens, and where was I going on holiday as she was going to Italy with her friend Jacky. Well, I guess I must have been too embarrassed to answer most of the questions as there is no evidence of any further correspondence. Well, what could I say? That I was a dedicated musician and occasional aluminium deckchair-maker who went to Middlesbrough for his holidays? I don't think she'd have been too impressed, somehow.

The Speakeasy had become London's most popular late night hangout for the "in-crowd". We'd read about it in the *Melody Maker*; an exclusive spot where the stars sat in darkened corners, then jammed till dawn. So, you can imagine our excitement when Cana arranged for us to play there. My imagination went into overdrive. Hendrix and Beck watching us from the bar, while Keith Moon chatted to Andrew Loog Oldham. Bevies of dolly birds dancing in an uninhibited and provocative manner in front of us as we brought the house down. Of course, it was nothing like that. We were booked on a Monday night to play to a small, uninterested bunch that spent more time at the bar than Rumpole of the Bailey. They looked like they'd just dined on melatonin. Even the rumour that Jimi Hendrix's roadie was in attendance proved to be unfounded. Another shattered illusion. We broke down our equipment in disappointed silence, with only the prospect of beans on toast to look forward to back at the flat.

Living upstairs from us in West Hampstead was a string bassist of considerable repute called Jeff Clyne. Of course, being immersed in the blues we were unaware of his standing until Bruce discovered that he'd played with Ronnie Scott and Tubby Hayes, two big names on the British Jazz scene. He and his wife Chris were always pleasant to us when we passed on the stairs, and taking note of the limited cooking smells wafting from our flat, sometimes invited us upstairs to watch them eat. We left only when the rumblings from our stomachs made conversation impossible. One evening as the Clynes tucked into something substantial, Jeff mentioned that he would be playing at the Hammersmith Odeon the following week. It transpired that this was part of a whole week of concerts known as Jazz Expo 67, featuring such names as Miles Davis, Archie Shepp, Thelonious Monk, Charles Lloyd, Bill Evans and Ben Webster. He had some complimentary tickets and would we like to go? Well, we had neither the knowledge nor the sophistication to appreciate this kind of music, but hey, it was a free night out, so we accepted.

Arriving at the Odeon, it transpired that luck had not dealt us a particularly good hand. The following night was given over to an American Folk Blues Festival featuring Son House, Bukka White, Little Walter, Hound Dog Taylor, Sonny Terry and Brownie McGee, Koko Taylor and Skip James. Bollocks! Why wasn't Jeff Clyne on that night? Instead, we had to endure an evening of old blokes playing saxophones. During the interval, we pooled our resources and made our way to the foyer to indulge in a shared packet of crisps washed down by a shared half pint of lager. As we bemoaned the fact that Jeff Clyne wasn't Willie Dixon, my attention was drawn to the guy on my left, who seemed to be undergoing a parallel experience:

'It's the same as that other bloke, what'shisname…Charlie Parkinson. He was on drugs. And he couldn't play a proper tune either!'

I took advantage of our continuing lean period by checking out the local landmarks. According to the sleeve notes on my Django albums, quite a few had been recorded at Decca studios. Jeff Clyne informed me that Decca was situated just off West End Lane, and right next to the Railway Hotel—just up the road, in fact. I was aware of the latter because its upstairs room had become Klooks Kleek, one of the famous London club venues. It held regular Tuesday and Thursday sessions, and anybody who was anybody played there. I did an immediate 'reccie', and noticed that the Crazy World of Arthur Brown was the next attraction.

Well, we were skint, but maybe we could help out with the equipment, or hide somewhere inside. Whilst I was weighing up the pros and cons of illegal entry, I found myself standing on the very steps that Django Reinhardt, Stephan Grapelli and the rest of the Hot Club of France had walked up on their way to record such classics as 'Undecided', 'Night And Day', 'Daphne' and of course 'Stomping At Decca'. Not to forget that John Mayall and The Bluesbreakers recorded all their albums here. I suddenly felt very close to musical history. Oh, and we did blag our way into the Arthur Brown gig.

Early one Sunday evening, Andy took us to see a friend of his called Steve York, a bass player who'd recently played with the legendary Graham Bond. Bond had earlier fronted his own outfit featuring Ginger Baker, Jack Bruce and Dick Heckstall-Smith (or Dick Oxtail-Soup as he was sometimes known). We were impressed. Mrs York showed us to her son's bedroom where he lay, smoking cigarettes, listening to 'sounds' and practicing his bass. Judging by his general state of repose, detached manner, and occasional manic laugh, it was obvious that he hadn't been sleeping off the effects of a large Sunday roast dinner and two halves of Courage Best. Even I could tell he was stoned.

A few days later we went to see him play with a band at the famed Ealing Blues Club, where he played a whole song with a fag in his mouth. It was like watching my dad on bass!

Some five years later I was invited to Richard Branson's newly-opened Manor Studios to take part in a jam-session which was organised by Steve, and released shortly after as Manor Live. I don't think anyone got paid, but we all got nicely out of it and made some good music, man. Come to think of it, we even had to pay towards the 'wacky-backy' and make our own way there and back home! Eee, we were keen them days.

Soon after, Steve joined a band called Vinegar Joe, which featured Elkie Brooks and Robert Palmer. Our paths crossed again a few years later on a TV session for Arthur Brown, strangely enough. This time Arthur Brown paid me for coming to see him! A number of years later I read that Steve been arrested on a bus for sexual assault. He claimed that he'd been high on LSD and was not wholly responsible for his actions. This cut no ice with the judge who found him guilty as charged. Sad.

In an effort to improve on our workload, we put together a demo-tape to persuade record companies to offer us a deal. Having set up our equipment in Andy's dining room, we were joined by Paul Kossoff and his little one-track tape machine. Acting as engineer, he placed the single microphone in position with a natural ease and confidence. Was there no end to this man's talent?! 'Rock Me Baby', 'The Walk', 'Get Ready', 'Early In The Morning', 'Getting Mighty Crowded', and an original, curiously titled '14th Story (Boulevard Suicide)' were captured on a small quarter-inch tape, though sadly, nothing came of it. On the inside of the lid, Bruce wrote: "Very rough tape all through a 50-watt amp with a cheap machine".

It was hardly the stuff to impress ruthless record moguls with, and whilst Cana Variety were securing more gigs, the camaraderie that held us together was beginning to fade. I guess that growing into young men had a lot to do with it. The naive youths were evolving into individual thinkers, and Paul in particular was becoming more remote, eschewing his razor and, for some curious reason, his socks, in an effort to discover those hidden depths. Living together was becoming increasingly difficult.

By October, Paul had decided to completely ignore both Bruce and myself, a tricky situation when you're sharing the same room, not to mention the same stage. My own disillusionment was exacerbated when a couple of recently purchased Segovia albums meant I fell in love with the sound of the classical guitar and resolved to find myself a teacher when I returned to Middlesbrough. Yep, I'd had enough. The end was nigh.

In the meantime, it was rumoured that Peter Green was looking for a bass player, so Bruce rang the man himself from the Borenious residence and requested an audition. For some reason, Peter brought his guitar over to Andy's place for a jam session! He also arrived with the relatively unknown Jeremy Spencer, thus transforming Golders Green's usual tranquil atmosphere into a little piece of Southside Chicago. Peter was impressed, but later that week it was announced that John McVie had quit Mayall's band to team up with Peter—yes, Fleetwood Mac.

Oh well.

But hang on—if McVie had quit Mayall's band, then who…?

Within hours, I found myself outside of a tall building near Paddington station. Bruce was ringing on the bell marked Mayall. A window on the fourth floor opened, and the face of the father of British blues peered down on us.

'Yes?' enquired the man himself, regarding the slightly undernourished duo with interest.

'I'm a bass player and this is my friend,' shouted Bruce excitedly. 'I'm looking for a gig.'

He must have felt sympathetic because he threw the front door key down to us and shouted out his flat number. We climbed the stairs with mounting excitement. John bloody Mayall!

His 'pad' was small but funky and lined with albums, which he seemed to play continuously. Mick Taylor sat quietly on a sofa, absorbing his mentor's choice of blues music, which would eventually stand him in good stead for his stint with the Rolling Stones. Our host was very hospitable and even made us a cup of tea. Yes, even blues legends like a nice cuppa. As we listened to the stream of blues emanating from the hi-fi, Bruce enquired after the bass playing spot in the Bluesbreakers. Alas, the situation was fulfilled and the poor lad looked crestfallen. It's tough at the bottom.

Needless to say, our conversation was limited on the train journey back to West Hampstead. We had little to look forward to and even less to eat. A schoolboy sitting opposite opened a packet of biscuits, then shuffled uneasily in his seat as I stared fixedly at his tempting snack. He disembarked hurriedly at the next stop. A few days later, we caught Fleetwood Mac at the Marquee, by hiding in (and on) the toilets to avoid detection. This would, of course, have resulted in a fine equal to the admission price, which was a luxury we could ill-afford. At this rate, my chin could soon require alternative means of support.

> If you can't leave in a taxi you can leave in a huff. If that's too soon, you can leave in a minute and a huff—Bert Kalmer /Groucho Marx.

Because of the "Paul situation", Bruce and I threw in the towel and cancelled the existing gigs. I took on a few cleaning jobs to help me through the final couple of weeks, romantically inspired by stories of Muddy Waters working as a janitor at Chess studios in Chicago during his early Sixties lean period. One assignment was to clean the flat of an elderly widow in Golders Green. She stood behind me throughout the entire operation, pointing out the bits I'd missed, then ordered me to walk her small terrier dog in a nearby park.

'Whatever you do, don't let him off the lead because he chases other dogs,' she barked. So did the dog—constantly. My reply was muttered and incomprehensible. Halfway round the park, having endured ten minutes of yapping and heaving, I released the stupid little bastard from its captive state. Big mistake. It shot off like a bat out of hell, in pursuit of anything canine. Its first challenge was a Great Dane; other breeds followed. Whenever I tried to intervene, it bared its teeth, then ran off to its next conquest, leaving me to apologise for its aggressive behaviour. Twenty minutes later, having endured the wrath of a dozen dog lovers, I finally managed to grab it by the scruff of the neck and leash it up. Once outside the park gates, it received a sharp kick up the arse. It yelped, then turned and looked up at me with a defiant stare.

'Son of a bitch!' I yelled.

'Correct!' it barked back.

Determined to stay out of trouble with the RSPCA, I choose to ignore its intimidatory stance. It responded by dragging me back to its resolute owner. It was a very lucky dog. Muddy Waters would have shot it.

Unsure of my immediate future, I decided to trade in the Marshall amplifier and speaker cabinet for something a little more portable. Paul Kossoff recommended a second-hand Fender Super combo which was sitting in Selmers. Whilst we were making the deal, I struck up a conversation with another customer, Dave Tedstone. It transpired that he was looking for a maple neck Telecaster like mine and was willing to make a straight swap with his own, a vintage model sporting a Gibson 'Humbucker' pickup. I had no hesitation in agreeing to his offer and we arranged to meet the following afternoon. Meanwhile, an excited Kossoff showed us Eric Clapton's psychedelic Gibson SG guitar, which was in for repair. We drooled in tandem. A few days later, on November 4th, I left London aboard the 2 p.m. train, having failed to make an impression in the "cut-throat world of pop".

Tables and Chairs

It felt strange to be back home. The damp north eastern night air, coupled with a sense of failure, brought about feelings of melancholy and isolation. The opportunity to sit alone in my bedroom gave me the time and space to assess my future; the longing to be a respected musician demanded a lot of thought. Suddenly, a voice appeared from nowhere.

'Boiled eggs, son?' enquired my mother from the foot of the stairs.

'Umm?' I responded weakly, attempting a return to earth. 'Oh, yea.'

She acknowledged my momentous decision and returned to the kitchen whilst I resumed my pondering.

I could hear my father's voice in another room. '...world of his own... get some sort of job...mumble-mumble.'

Picking up my Telecaster, I let fly with a flurry of notes in D-minor, that saddest of all keys. Building up to a climactic finish, I leapt to my feet, emotionally charged and filled with artistic repression, ready to satisfy my inner feelings. I threw back my head, closed my eyes, my soul stirring with primitive passion, ready to squeeze every last ounce of expression from that final note. It never came.

My bloody eggs were ready.

Making contact with old friends was an obvious way of settling in, and after phone calls to Joe Bradley and a few old chums, I made my way to the Purple Onion coffee bar to gather my thoughts. The 'Onion' was an established meeting place for the hipper element and local characters—the only remaining part of the legendary Mr McCoys club, that late night hangout for after-gig Road Runners' discussions. The eldest McCoy brother, John, had established the nearby Kirklevington Country Club, an acknowledged landmark on the Sixties northern club scene. The youngest, Eugene, was an old school friend, whose good-natured banter endeared him to most. As we chatted over coffee, he brought me up to date with the local news and gossip, encouraged me to form my own band, and then tried to sell me a paisley kipper tie. I settled for another coffee and promised to consider the latter.

All music is folk music, I ain't never heard no horse sing a song
                                                    —*Louis Armstrong.*

I wasted no time in satisfying my desire to take classical guitar lessons. According to *BMG* (Banjo, Mandolin and Guitar) Magazine, my nearest classical guitar teacher lived in Stockton, and was called Gladys V. Goldsbrough (nee Kirkham) L.R.A.M. A.R.C.M L.T.C.I. She offered me an initial course of ten lessons at four guineas, plus ten shillings for the tutor, which was a yet another Mel Bay publication. God, that guy had it sewn up!

The next step was to visit Hamiltons and purchase a nylon string guitar. Being financially challenged, I finally settled for a model from the 'cheaper range' called a Giannini, which was actually quite playable. As luck would have it, my mother had retained the original 'nuns habit' guitar bag and I experienced a feeling of déjà vu, albeit on a different bus route.

It was quite a culture shock to renounce a rock'n'roll lifestyle in favour of a guitar teacher called Gladys. My initial intentions were honourable enough, but it wasn't long before the Telecaster was back out of its case. I was left with a momentous decision. Should I be a rock-influenced classical guitarist, or a classically-influenced rock musician? In any event, thoughts of fusing the two styles helped take my mind off the impending possibility of a day job. This was a daunting prospect, yet par for the course if you're destined to be a dedicated 'artiste' whose influences included Howlin' Wolf's guitarist Hubert Sumlin, Jeff Beck, Django Reinhardt, and Gladys V. Goldsbrough (nee Kirkham) L.R.A.M. A.R.C.M. L.T.C.I..

It seemed obvious that success could only be achieved through serious effort and an honest existence. George Bernard Shaw's quote that "Hell is full of musical amateurs" was a good enough maxim to contemplate, even if it meant wearing two hats. Consequently, I persevered with elementary Bach via Gladys, and then took the first steps towards rock and roll rehabilitation by deciding to form a band. A new year was approaching and this resolution was totally natural, or should I say, essential. Reflecting on the past twelve months, the emphasis pointed towards progression and experience, key elements which would stand me in good stead for 1968.

Early in January, and with more than a little help from Eugene, I managed to gain access to an upstairs room at the Purple Onion (the paisley kipper tie decision was still on hold) and together with a local singer/character named Stooky, pulled together a bassist and drummer to churn out some maximum R&B. The first rehearsal went well, though Stooky's lurching deportment was light years away from my delusions de Rod Stewart. Having just recently parted company with Paul Rodgers, it was always going to be a hard act to follow, but I was relieved to see Stooky was at least wearing socks. Eugene, who was in attendance and had his own aspirations to front a soul band, shared some of the excitement that teenagers experience on their road to self-expression and enjoyment. I suggested Junior Wells' version of 'Hound Dog' to start and steamed in headfirst. It was great to play again and the guys were good. By the end of the night we were searching for a name—never an easy chore. The room we were using was stacked with tables and chairs, due perhaps to a surplus or, more likely, to create some space for us to set up our equipment. During one of those moments when people are deep in thought and you can almost hear their brains ticking over, Stooky suddenly made a suggestion:

'How about Tables and Chairs?'

We shot each other supportive glances, then nodded our approval.

Why not? 'Tables and Chairs?'

It was the Sixties after all, and there were dafter band names than that around. Sorted.

TABLES AND CHAIRS—END OF REHEARSAL JOKE
'Same time tomorrow, fellow Tables and Chairs member?'
'Only if I can be the chairman.'
'OK, I'll table that motion.'

On the second night, John McCoy paid us a visit. I assumed that he was in the vicinity and had just popped in for a quick listen, but he stayed for quite a while; he had a good ear for music. His band The Real McCoy, and prior to that, The Crawdaddies, had once been local scene-stealers, though they were now apparently on the wane. They'd released a single, an odd bluebeat-style ditty entitled 'Show Me How To Milk A Cow' and its dismal failure was probably the final nail in the coffin. Still, maybe he could help Tables and Chairs establish themselves with a few choice gigs.

My wishes took a more realistic turn when John suggested that I meet him the next day in the Purple Onion—an invitation I readily accepted. Eugene looked very pleased with himself. Maybe he'd just off-loaded another Kipper tie. Stooky lit up yet another cigarette and inhaled deeply. Due to his habit of holding his fag in an inverted fashion, between thumb and forefinger, there was so much nicotine on his fingers that it looked like he was wearing a rust-coloured glove. I lit up a Disque Blue and exhaled a French-flavoured sigh of contentment, remembering to avoid the Stooky-grip. Ah, tres bon.

Lunchtime at the Purple Onion was an education in itself. Office workers, businessmen, students, shady characters and musicians, mingled in the smoky atmosphere amid snacks and meals, served up by yet more McCoy brothers; Peter and Tom, an eccentric pair with a rather camp approach. John's arrival was acknowledged with an unspoken respect. He possessed the charisma of someone in the know; been there, seen it, done it. After the usual pleasantries, he came straight to the point.

'I'm really into putting together a band with a big blues influence, y'know, with a West Coast feel,' he explained.

'I'd like you to be in it, along with the two Terry's from The Real McCoy. I think it could be good, what do you reckon?'

'Erm, yes… right,' I replied with uncertain assurance.

I inhaled a Players Number 6 and tried to look cool. Unfortunately, the smoke drifted into my eyes and activated my tear ducts. John, sensing an emotional reaction, placed a reassuring hand on my shoulder and ordered a sweet tea to aid my apparent disposition. It occurred to me that if I played my cards right and faked a complete emotional breakdown, I might even get a cheese sandwich out of it. However, rational thinking and personal pride prevented it.

The other guys in Tables and Chairs took it on the chin and accepted my unexpected career move. At least I think they did. Perhaps now, over thirty-seven years later, they still bear a grudge and blame me for two wasted nights of rehearsal time. Sorry, lads!

I'd been a subscriber to *Beat Instrumental* magazine for a few years. It was the only publication that was directed towards the rock musician, with features such as 'Player of the Month' and 'In the Studio'. A quick perusal of the February edition enlightened me to the fact that the Blue Horizon label was releasing a single by 'the Chicken Shack' called 'It's O.K. With Me, Baby'. It featured "the group's girl singer and pianist Christine Perfect, who also wrote the song. Peter Greens' Fleetwood Mac also had their first LP planned for release on the same label in the near future, and there were plans to record visiting American Bluesman Eddie Boyd".

In the same magazine, a letter to the 'YOUR QUERIES ANSWERED' column asked:

Dear Gary,

Being in a group that plays Cream and Hendrix-type numbers, I am a great fan of Eric Clapton and Jimi Hendrix's lead work. Would I be too inquisitive if I asked how Eric gets that weird fantastic sound from his amplifier? I have also noted that Jeff Beck and Mick Taylor (Bluesbreakers) have the same sound. As far as I can see it might be a mixture of fuzz and a very high Treble Booster. In your April issue in an article called 'The Sounds I Like' by Britain's top guitarists, Eric Clapton said that he had taken the covers off his pickup, and this sounded a good idea. On my guitar, a Harmony H 75, this is impossible and so I was thinking of taking off one of them to fit a good quality pickup on, one that I could take the cover off. If it proves a success and better than my own pickup then I could convert the others. Could you suggest a pickup and what would be the price?
BARRY HODSON
Ellesmere Port, Cheshire.

ANSWER: Eric Clapton gets his distinctive guitar sound by a combination of things. He plays a very good guitar with extremely powerful pickups coupled to a first class Marshall amplifier. He has also perfected his own technique of obtaining feedback from his guitar to speaker that gives him a sustained note and, of course, he is a brilliant guitarist in a class of his own. Jeff Beck also has top class gear similar to Clapton's and again uses a lot of volume to give his guitar a certain amount of feedback tendency. He also sometimes uses fuzz to very good effect. Certainly, when he was with the Yardbirds, some of his sounds were quite incredible, often resembling instruments such as sitar, cello, violin, etc.
Jimi Hendrix uses many electronic aids as you will have read in last month's issue (page 13) but he is far from being an 'electronic guitarist' relying

purely on his gimmick effects—he is one of the country's top guitarists as are
Clapton, Beck and Mick Taylor.
I don't think that you would benefit from adding a fresh pickup to your guitar
as it is equipped with very good quality pickups as standard and I feel sure
that with the use of a good fuzz unit you will be able to obtain the sound you
require with a bit of experiment.

Did Barry ever achieve tonal satisfaction, or did he become just another frustrated guitarist? I wonder. Maybe he changed his name to Brian May or Dave Hill. Did he take heed of Gary's advice and purchase a fuzz unit? We'll probably never know. Oh, and did a certain guitarist from Middlesbrough ever become Player of the Month? Yes, in August 1977.

The Real McCoy had a few gigs left to honour and John, eager to establish our new relationship, invited me along to one of them to 'have a blow'. Though the band featured legendary sax player Ron Aspery, they really were past their sell-by date, and those members who weren't half-cut seemed disinterested. They also featured a rather odd keyboard player with an unfortunate pudding-basin hairstyle who was laughingly referred to as Grocer Jack, a character from a silly Manfred Mann song called 'My Name Is Jack'. John asked me up on stage and I obliged. Having very little in common with the others regarding disinterest and inebriation, I approached my solo like a man possessed—I'd show 'em! I think they were impressed, though it was hard to tell amid all that disinterest and inebriation. The band's drummer, Terry Popple, who'd helped out the Road Runners in their hour of need, seemed to enjoy the 'jam' and later recalled Dave Usher's Veno's night.

'Is 'e still on the medication?' he joked.

'Worse—'es on the beer!' I replied.

We were joined by the bass player, Terry Sidgewick, a bit of a cheeky charmer with a penchant for flashy shirts.

'Alright, Road Runner?' he enquired, showing off his trademark grin. He'd referred to me in this manner once before, when I was a Road Runner. I suppose I'd have to join another band to lose that particular title. As luck would have it, I wouldn't have long to wait.

Grade Two Professional

By 1968, the word 'progressive' was still the only definition any musician or hip fan wanted to be associated with. Freddie and the Dreamers, along with Malcolm Cairns, were a distant blur on the horizon, unaware of such musical innovations as Spirit, Captain Beefheart and his Magic Band, the Mothers of Invention and the Grateful Dead. Or maybe Malcolm, still smarting from his premature dismissal from the Road Runners, had grown waist-length hair, moved to LA and was sitting-in from time to time with Blood Sweat and Tears.

I was still in touch with Bruce Thomas, and his recent correspondence had charted his progress. Apparently he'd joined a band with the silliest name yet—The Yellow Passion Loaf (seems Tables And Chairs wasn't that bad after all)—but as a career move he was on a hiding to nothing. I came to this conclusion via a letter from Andy Borenious, which described Bruce's new friends as "sick hips, sort of switched-on jet setters, (they're) very thick despite their pretensions. They say things like 'Blues is dead'—typical groupies. I don't know what Bruce is doing among them. Another good man down the acid plughole, never to appear again. Very sad".

Fortunately, Andy's assessment was wrong and Bruce eventually tasted success with the Sutherland Brothers and Quiver before becoming an Attraction for Elvis Costello. The same letter also gave an early indication of Paul Rodgers' blossoming career, describing a gig with his band, Brown Sugar, at the Fickle Pickle club in Finsbury Park, as "absolutely fantastic". Dave Usher, in a hurry to prove his worth, had apparently signed a binding contract that prevented him working as a paid musician for some time to come. Ouch! To counteract his despondency, he made an executive decision to ride out the offending sentence by registering as a full time lorry driver. Joe must have been both proud and saddened.

Tramline, as we had chosen to call ourselves, made their debut at the Kirk in early February, followed a few days later by a gig at the Sacred Heart Church Hall, Middlesbrough. Eugene's outfit, The New Elastic Band, was supporting along with Chelfont Line, completing a bill that cost the punter the sum of five shillings. To help publicise our world premiere, The *Evening Gazette* interviewed John McCoy, featuring a piece of creative journalism. Apparently, Manfred Mann had shown interest in the band and was keen to become involved in both recording and management.

Really? It was the first I'd heard of it.

"This might also mean a residency at the Marquee Club and we're very exited at the prospect, because it's one of London's top clubs," John was quoted as saying. The crossing of fingers took place in at least three separate households.

John Peel's radio show, *Top Gear*, produced some great live sessions, including Cream, Jeff Beck Group and Peter Green's Fleetwood Mac—all great guitar groups. I recorded a few on our Grundig TK 20 one-track reel-to-reel domestic recorder with the microphone jammed firmly up against the tiny speaker. Anyone entering the room was shushed into silence, though occasionally the family dog could be heard barking for a few seconds before a 'Shudup!' and/or a whack from one of the family curtailed his efforts. I would grit my teeth and roll my eyes, then curse the dumb creature under my breath for being insensitive.

Though I still managed to avoid the Kipper tie, Eugene's next offer was too good to refuse. A well-tailored paisley shirt ("made in London, ex-Alan Bown Set... honest".) for only two pounds. Very, very nice and thank you. I turned up at the next Tramline gig proudly displaying my new acquisition, confident in my appearance and ready to roll. Unfortunately, John recognised the shirt as one that he'd lent to his enterprising younger brother some months previously and was not amused. To his credit, he never brought the matter up again and I got my money's worth, even wearing it to impress Gladys V. Goldsbrough (nee Kirkham) L.R.A.M. A.R.C.M. L.T.C.I. at one of her lessons. I would over the next six months find myself rigged out by the same means, acquiring a two-tone red velvet jacket and a material-matching purple bow tie.

Professional men, they have no cares;
Whatever happens, they get theirs—Ogden Nash.

My dedication to my vocation meant that anything serious regarding the opposite sex was, apart from the odd dalliance, secondary. I was in no particular hurry. Without making too much of an issue out of the whole thing, I had in fact become a professional musician, that is to say, one who can exist on monies earned from one particular source. This wasn't The Wildflowers 'starving in a garret' style. No, it was much more civilised and far less painful. And we had a proper van—a Ford Transit long wheelbase model with a couple of armchairs in the back! I was a bachelor, living at home and earning regular, if not big money. Though the Manfred Mann rumours subsided, McCoy, ever the entrepreneur, had arranged a meeting with Chris Blackwell, head of Island Records. They were, by then, an up-and-coming company, which boasted a respected roster of artists including Traffic, Spooky Tooth, Jimmy Cliff and Wynder K. Frogg (aka Mick Weaver, an organist from Bolton). However, a demo tape would be required before securing any sort of recording agreement.

Recording studios were not exactly big business in the north east in 1968. Along with companies marketing Conservative Party car stickers, Rugby Union players and fanatical Tramline supporters, they were considered somewhat rare. Undeterred, we were advised that Impulse Studios in Wallsend-On-Tyne was our best bet—it was "fully sound-proofed and capable of handling ten musicians." How could they possibly manage that? Did they have a free bar and loose women? Apparently not. All you needed was a custom-built console incorporating an 8-channel stereo mixer, four channels of reverb, two channels of echo, plus Shure Unisphere and AKG D19 mikes. We booked an early-evening-till-midnight session, which we considered adequate enough to capture the sound and style of Tramline. Proprietor-cum-engineer Dave Wood helped us set up and informed us that his recording machines were Wear and Wright Series 6H, which ran at 15 ips. I nodded off at that point, but woke up in time to hear him waxing lyrical about a local singer-songwriter, Alan Hull.

'We've had people in from London and Scotland. Coloured Rain have been in too,' he enthused. 'They're off to the Continent soon.'

By the end of the session we had three or four songs 'in the can'. The rest was down to John and his powers of persuasion.

I still found myself leading a musical double-life; a natural rock and blues personality existing side by side with an alter ego of amateur classical guitarist. A night of Telecaster-bashing sometimes preceded a calm morning in Gladys' sitting room, where I could furrow my brow to works by Sor, Giuliani, or Bach. The majority of her students seemed to be schoolchildren or adults with sensible jobs. On one of my visits, I had a brief chat to the preceding pupil, another guitar hopeful.

'Did you have a good lesson?' I enquired.

'Not bad,' he answered. 'I'm on grade five—what grade are you on?'

'Oh, just grade two,' I replied, removing my guitar from its case.

'Oh, really,' he responded loftily. 'Well I must go, I'm on the two till ten shift at the foundry. Don't you have a job then?'

'Yes,' I confirmed. 'I'm a professional musician.' He gave me a perplexed look.

'Which instrument?' he inquired, as Gladys called me in.

'The guitar,' I answered nonchalantly. He attempted a reply but failed.

Tramline made its debut at the renowned Marquee Club in London on April 6th, supporting Ten Years After, the future supergroup led by guitar-meister Alvin Lee. The occasion was even more memorable as it was the tenth anniversary of the club's existence. Alvin was amiable, as were the rest of the band. They had no problem sharing the limited space that was the dressing room with the humble support band. Alvin even inquired after my vintage Telecaster, comparing it quite rightly with the one played by the other Lee, Chris Farlowe's guitarist, Albert. It was a dead ringer, Gibson pickup et al. The audience response to our set was appreciative but cool; they were there to see Alvin and the boys, who were great. Their version of the classic 'Woodchopper's Ball' was a show-stopper that allowed the guys to stretch to their limits; a basic twelve-bar blues performed with great character—Woodstock, here we come. After the show I gazed at the poster announcing that month's attractions, which would now be regarded as a who's who of classic British rock and blues: Jeff Beck; The Crazy World Of Arthur Brown; John Mayall; The Bonzo Dog Doo Dah Band; The Who; Long John Baldry; Manfred Mann; Spencer Davis Group and Traffic. Ee, we didn't know we were born!

Our lodgings that night were supplied by a girl called Pat, one of John's old friends from Middlesbrough, who resided in a flat on Shoot Up Hill, a main thoroughfare between Cricklewood and Kilburn. Today's cynical attitudes would suggest that the route was littered with heroin addicts, but in truth it was just a respectable part of London. Pat shared the two-bedroom ground floor flat with a guy called Bob, an amiable chap whose taste in music was similar to ours. His only failing was a habit of bending down to adjust the stereogram whilst wearing a rather short dressing gown. I'm sure that his enthusiasm for providing us with the best possible tonal qualities was uppermost in his mind, but an early morning viewing of his exposed scrotum tended to detract one's attention from the music. We closed our eyes and thought about the money we were saving on hotel bills.

All you need in this life is ignorance and confidence: then success is sure—
Mark Twain.

John McCoy's powers of persuasion finally bore fruit when the band was offered an album deal with Island Records. Not only that, Chris Blackwell—the boss man himself—was to produce it. Tempered by a certain ignorance, I took it all in my stride, as I'm sure the others did. Hell, if I were offered that kind of deal today, I'd consider myself privileged. In retrospect, my working relationships at the time were bordering on the surreal: Chris Blackwell one day, Gladys V. Goldsbrough (nee Kirkham) L.R.A.M. A.R.C.M. L.T.C.I. the next.

It was around this period that I started to become more health conscious, an attitude brought about through lunchtime discussions in the Purple Onion. I'd always been a disciple of Newboulds, local purveyors of fine saveloys, but the opening of Middlesbrough's first health food shop gave me new food for thought. Both sunflower and pumpkin seeds became my staple snack diet, which encouraged non-believers to accuse me of eating rabbit food. Peasants! As my alcohol and tobacco intake was extremely moderate, a good kick-about in the park posed no problems whatsoever. I always put myself forward for a game whenever possible, often fuelled by seeded energy and wholewheat scones. We'd dazzle the strollers in Albert Park with short bursts of skill and long periods of mediocrity, interspersed with fag-breaks. Afterwards, we'd reward ourselves by commandeering a rowing boat on the small, murky lake. Happy days.

I acquired of a cheap Egmond steel string acoustic guitar with a string-action only marginally lower than Old Butterfly's. Though inadequate for any sort of serious performance, it was perfect for slide playing, where the notes are sounded by the use of a metal or glass tube slipped onto one of the smaller digits of the left hand. Natural curiosity had opened my eyes to 'open' guitar tunings, especially those used by slide guitar virtuosos Robert Johnson and Elmore James. Those two boys had style and influence. Though I'd dabbled with the slide or 'bottleneck' style, I'd never gone the whole hog. Now I had the time, the attitude and the opportunity to put it to the test.

Message implanted in brain—May 9th 1968
Tomorrow you are playing at the Marquee Club in London supporting the Aynsley Dunbar Retaliation. John suggests you bring along the acoustic slide guitar to perform a solo piece.

I took it all in my stride. Well, you do when you're only seventeen, don't you? At the required moment, I sat down on the edge of the stage, picked up my junk guitar (now tuned to the chord of G-major) and drifted off into the Mississippi Delta. Marvellous really, apart from one important factor. I'd given no thought at all to the amplification. The Marquee crowd of the Sixties was there for one thing only—the music. It was a soft drinks only policy that was never questioned, unlike the antics of M.C. John Gee.

'That's a lovely velvet bow-tie you're wearing, young man,' he announced whilst seeking serious eye contact with me.

'Erm, I bought it from the singer's brother,' I replied, looking at the floor. Sailor, beware! Though I tried, the audience's hearing capabilities were pushed to the limit until McCoy leaped forward with his vocal microphone to save the day, kneeling unceremoniously in front of me in order to capture the moment. Blues from the Tees Delta, indeed! I'd given my first solo slide guitar performance. It was to be the first of many.

Another regular customer at the Purple Onion noted this serious interest in slide guitar playing. He was a student at Middlesbrough College of Art, a bespectacled lad whose dress sense rarely stretched beyond a donkey jacket and loon pants. The David Coverdale of 1968 bore little resemblance to the future rock star. Dave (as he was then known) was kind enough to lend me his Stefan Grossman plays Bottleneck Blues LP complete with explanatory booklet. I gave it one listen, decided Mr Grossman was lacking in character and returned it to its owner. Nevertheless, we struck up a friendship that would eventually bring me fame and… well, fame. But that's another story.

Membership of Tramline also meant free membership to Kirklevington Country Club—a nice little perk. Sunday nights saw top line acts performing on the small stage and I'd be there whenever possible, craning my neck to catch a glimpse of established and future stars. Memorable performances included those by Jeff Beck's Group featuring Rod Stewart, Jethro Tull, Terry Reid, Joe Cocker and the Grease Band, the Bonzo Dog Doo Dah Band and Spooky Tooth. Saturday nights were handed over to DJ Tony Hargan, whose tasty collection of discs encouraged the lubricated throng to display some rather uninhibited dance-floor cavortings. A small group of West Indians led by a pleasant fellow called Lashly, performed dance routines never before seen in rural north Yorkshire. Their twirls, leaps and lurches were given added impetus by the legendary 'Lashly Drop'. Here, a handkerchief would be placed ceremoniously on the floor, prompting Lashly to fall forward into a press-up position. He would then pick up the serviette between his teeth and bounce back up without missing a beat. A chorus of 'De drinks is on Lashly!' would precede a Trinidadian exodus to the bar for another round of Carlsberg Specials.

A MIDDLESBROUGH JOKE

An unemployed man was walking past a pub one day, when he caught sight of a sign in the window. It read: A PIE, A PINT, AND A WOMAN FOR THE NIGHT—£1. Unable to control his curiosity, he entered the bar and enquired as to the validity of such an offer. The barman, nonchalantly wiping a pint glass with a tea towel, pointed out that due to a new promotion from the brewery, a pie, a pint of your choice, and a woman of easy virtue could indeed be had for just one pound. Rubbing his chin, the man gave the offer some serious consideration, then inquired: 'What kind of pies are they?'

Tramline's repertoire consisted mainly of R&B covers such as 'Statesboro Blues', 'Look Over Yonder Wall' and 'Killing Floor', combined with contemporary West Coast favourites like 'Hey Grandma' by Moby Grape and 'Love Me Two Times' by the Doors. Though we tried to slot in the odd original, songwriting was not the band's forte. I'd manage to incorporate a bit of my ever-developing slide playing on 'Statesboro', but my overall style was of a British blues-rocker with a touch of Steve Cropper thrown in. My classical guitar training remained a personal challenge and was unlikely to figure in Tramline's plans. My main concern remained the lack of original material, exacerbated by the impending recording sessions for Island. Skates would need to be attached to feet pretty sharpish.

Prior to my return home from London, I'd made an album swap with Paul Kossoff. In exchange for a B.B.King LP, Paul gave me Segovia's Granada featuring works by Asquado, Sor, Ponce, Tansman, Albenez and Granados. I was a little surprised at his eagerness to part with this album as, according to the back cover, it was an important memento. A hand-written message read: 'To Paul Kossoff. A souvenir of your first stage appearance—The Brady Ramblers, Prince Charles Theatre, March 1st—15th, 1964.' Other performers such as The Haverim and John Koster had also added their monikers to the occasion. The exchange was to prove fruitful for me. I still possess the Segovia album and eventually found another copy of the B.B. King record. Unknowingly, the former was to play a small part in the outcome of the forthcoming album.

John, being the most imaginative, began to make suggestions for the recording, which prompted me to make an attempt at the progressive. Because of its unusual melody, one particular track on Granada stood out. According to the liner notes, "'Mazurka' by Tansman was written for Segovia in Paris in 1925. Set with a sure knowledge of the resources of the guitar, it is a pleasant fusing of the elements of his native Polish dance-form with a mild bi-tonalism." Perfect for Tramline I thought!

I set about re-arranging the original to suit the band and came up with an inspirational gem (or so I thought). Our new version would include a drum solo! (Well, it seemed like a good idea at the time.)

Recording details were finally issued and we were advised to assemble at the very recently opened Morgan Studios in Willesden High Road in London. An exorbitant creative period of three days was set aside for us to complete our side of the bargain. Needless to say, we wouldn't hang out at too many clubs, pubs or restaurants during our visit. The studio's advertisement was headed by the statement:

"WE WANT TO PUT IT ON RECORD …newest, friendliest studio in London—8 track, mono, inspiration, everything."

Inspiration? In retrospect, I'd say that producer Chris Blackwell supplied a lot of that. Everything? Well, they had a hot drinks machine. Still, I suppose they were instrumental in helping Island 'put it on record', so credit where it's due. It was to be my first 'proper recording' and provided me with invaluable experience.

Somewhere Down the Line

To celebrate my elevated status to recording artist, I invested in some new equipment courtesy of a trip to Hamiltons. I cast a cursory glance at the window display of local bands' business cards, then headed upstairs to the big money department. Amongst the usual array of amplifiers was an impressive looking black 'stack' into which was plugged a sunburst Stratocaster. Without hesitation, I strapped it on and let fly with a few licks. The front panel of the amp was basic; just volume, treble, and bass, but it had a nice 'chunky' sound (as *Beat Instrumental* would have said). The assistant was over like a shot to start his sales pitch:

"…very high quality amplifier which employs the use of C-core transformers and produces 100 watts of undistorted power, and the standing noise level is 75mV across 15 ohms. Also…."

In the end I think I only bought it to shut him up. Twenty minutes later, an Impact 100 watt amplifier and two 4x12 speaker cabinets were in my possession. Full legal ownership would be mine after twelve monthly payments of fourteen pounds, sixteen shillings and threepence. I received of forty-three pounds and nine shillings in part exchange for my existing amplification, and yes, my long-suffering dad had to sign the hire purchase forms. My amplification, when strategically stacked, was taller than I was! To echo Muddy Waters' sentiment, I was ready. Ready, ready as I could be.

We travelled to London and recorded the album in the allocated three days and believe me, it sounds like we recorded it in the allocated three days. Retrospect is a marvellous thing—I just wish I'd known about it then. The track listing was as follows:

Harpoon Man
National Blues

Sorry Sorry
Look Over Yonder Wall
Rock And Roll Woman
Somewhere Down The Line
Mazurka
Statesboro Blues
Killing Floor

A BRIEF RETROSPECTIVE CRITIQUE OF THE ABOVE

HARPOON MAN—A cover of a song I'd never heard before or since, which was given a Yardbirds-type treatment. Slightly manic in its delivery.

NATIONAL BLUES—An original instrumental slide guitar tune performed by myself along with ex-Road Runner Bruce Thomas on double bass. I'd borrowed a National steel-bodied guitar from Bruce's friend Mike Absalom, hence the title.

SORRY SORRY—A band original. An attempt at a slow Chicago blues in the style of Buddy Guy et al.

LOOK OVER YONDER WALL.—The classic Elmore James song given a 'Green Onions'-type treatment.

ROCK AND ROLL WOMAN—A rather pointless attempt at the Buffalo Springfield original with a dodgy guitar solo.

SOMEWHERE DOWN THE LINE—A cover of a Little Johnny Taylor song that featured Terry Sidgewick on lead vocals. Under-produced.

MAZURKA—Yes, that aforementioned Polish folk tune with the drum solo. I made a ricket, but due to embarrassment, refused to acknowledge it. I still have to live with it! Overall, a nervous attempt at a strange choice.

STATESBORO BLUES—The band's version of Taj Mahal's version of the Blind Willie McTell song. Dynamically redundant.

KILLING FLOOR—A cover of a Howlin' Wolf classic which would soon be given superior treatments by both Electric Flag and Jimi Hendrix.

Hindsight is a great thing of course. At the time I just plugged in and played—full stop. When the engineer started talking about overdubs, drop-ins and individual foldback, my eyes just glazed over; I just presumed that you played live, as I'd done at Impulse in Wallsend. All in all, the end result could have been better. On the positive side, we received no known complaints from guardians of Polish folk tunes.

As we were packing away our equipment, Chris Blackwell took John aside and paid over our cash advance of one hundred pounds. Two hours later, my quarter share was nestling inside the till at the famous Take 6 boutique in Wardour Street. Twenty-eight years later, the album was re-released on CD and I was asked to write the liner notes. I accepted the challenge and provided the record company, Demon, with a credible effort, even submitting items of archive memorabilia from my personal collection. Six months later, due to disappointing sales, 'Somewhere Down the Line' was deleted for the second time.

My love life had been pretty uninspiring, due to a lack of enthusiasm on my part (or maybe my parts), though I did have a fling with a local vamp whose experience was obviously superior to mine. In fact, she even had her own custom pheromone made by the local chemist. The liaison proved to be disastrous, and she ran off with an ugly man. This in turn led me to seek solace in my music, an economy-size bag of Pontefract Cakes, and a hairdressing appointment. The latter was undertaken at Maurice Coiffeurs, an establishment operating from the now defunct Mr McCoys club. Here, crimpers offered the refined customer the latest in French and English styles. Maurice, a local lad, pursued an image of up-marketness, complete with pseudo French accent, though familiarity could easily lower his defences, especially on the telephone:

"allo, Maureece Kwaafer speaking. 'ow can I 'elp yoo?'

'Oh, hello Maurice, it's Mick Moody here, can you fit me in?'

'Oh, hello mate, how's it going. Usual trim is it?'

'Yes please.'

'OK. Two o'clock Thursday, ta-ra.' C'est la vie.

The band's usual circuit stretched from Northumberland, through Durham and down to south Yorkshire, with an occasional foray into the Midlands. If the venue was near home, we could satisfy our digestive cravings by visiting a late night Indian restaurant, situated in one of the less selective parts of town. Here, drunken morons would sometimes attract the waiter's attention by yelling. 'Oow Sabu, ger us a fuckin' steak and chips with all the trimmings—now.' The abused Asian would offer a small bow and smile, secure in the knowledge that 'the trimmings' would include a generous amount of phlegm and a quick wipe-over with the toilet brush.

The band had dealings with another Asian; a bright, ambitious lad who fancied his chances as a promoter. As a gesture of goodwill, he invited the band and their wives/girlfriends to dinner at the family home, where we ate a sociable curry, served in style by various members of the household. After dinner, things were going as well as could be expected in such a mixed gathering, when the entrance of the fellow's younger sister, bedecked from head to toe in a traditional sari, halted the conversation. Smiling, she walked a few paces then treated us to a quick twirl.

'This is what all the girls wear back home in India,' announced the proud father.

We all nodded our approval and smiled. All except Terry Sidgewick that is, whose keen powers of observation differed somewhat to the rest of us.

'You'd have a job getting your hand away in that!' he gleefully informed us. His wife shot him a look that spoke volumes—and ultimately, divorce. Those that weren't embarrassed, bit their lips. We were never asked back.

July saw Tramline heading somewhere down the A1 to support Jethro Tull at the Marquee Club. More importantly, our attendance was required at a photo session at the studios of renowned photographer Gered Mankowitz, celebrated son of the famous writer, Wolf. The object of the exercise was to capture a pose good enough to adorn the back cover of the album. Our optimism-meter registered 100, though Terry Sidgwick's carefree attitude was, as always, an inspiration.

Mr Mankowitz's trendy mews location was totally in keeping with the image bestowed upon Sixties snappers, courtesy of David Bailey and David Hemmings' Blow-up caricature. I'm not so sure what he really thought of us, but as Island artists, we would surely command at least a modicum of respect. He did his best. The finished product portrayed a bunch of individuals that posed no serious threat to Peter Frampton and other 'faces of '68'. Brief character descriptions are as follows:

John McCoy—Distant expression and ill-fitting shirt. Evidence of developing love handles.

Terry Sidgwick—That which is visible is presentable.

Terry Popple—Looks like a man with a hangover.

Yours Truly—A face that ponders the distinct possibility of terminal mumps. Sad hairstyle (arguably Maurice's creation).

I doubt very much that we made it into the Gered Mankowitz Collection.

Tramline never had a roadie, so to speak. We couldn't really afford one, so we just got on with the job ourselves, though on London jaunts the volunteers seemed to come out of the woodwork. Local characters would cue up to accompany us to a prestigious gig to 'help out', even though their knowledge of stage presentation was minimal. One such enthusiast, who accompanied the band on this particular outing, was to test Mankovitz's patience to the limit. As we adopted the suggested poses in readiness for the shot, the fool in question started making suggestions of his own. This eventually caused so much displeasure that he was threatened with swift ejection. Once the shoot was over, we made our way to the Marquee. A quick stroll down Wardour Street presented the same likely lad with an opportunity to diminish the stocks of Take 6 by nearly twenty five percent. He left the shop looking like the Michelin X man, covered from neck to ankle in stolen goods. By the time he reached the club, he was sweating like a racehorse.

'Fuckin' idiots down 'ere,' he concluded. 'Too busy posin' to notice.'

That night he became, sartorially speaking, the most multifarious roadie the Marquee Club had ever witnessed. John Gee was chomping at the bit.

A few weeks later we were back at the Marquee supporting Tim Rose, an American singer-songwriter. Rose had risen to prominence through his brooding arrangement of 'Hey Joe', inspiring a certain Jimi Hendrix to take it a step further. Since then, he'd established a respectful following through songs like 'Morning Dew', which the Jeff Beck Group covered on their *Truth* album. Drumming with him that night was John Bonham, giving one of his final performances as an unknown. Earlier that day, whilst taking a casual stroll down Gerard Street, I spotted Paul Rodgers on the opposite pavement. He was armed with a bucket of water and a ladder, which was soon propped up against a wall and parallel to a large dusty window. Given the circumstances I decided it unwise to attempt a reconciliation.

Distraction from Tramline's travels came in the shape of a practical examination judged by, yes, you've guessed it, Gladys V. Goldsbrough (nee Kirkham) L.R.A.M. A.R.C.M. L.T.C.I.. The Royal Schools of Music test of practical ability consisted of six important aspects and required the candidate to secure at least one hundred out of the one hundred and fifty marks on offer. My efforts were rewarded with merit and were recorded as follows:

SCALES AND ARPEGGIOS—24 out of 27
Scales were well known, apart from a slip or two in minors. Arpeggios well done.
PIECE 1; SARABANDE FROM THIRD LUTE SUITE BY BACH—25 out of 30
There were some unclear moments in this, and a few small inaccuracies in notes. But on the whole it was well done, with pleasant tone.
PIECE 2; MINUET FROM SONATA NO I BY DIABELLI—24 out of 30
Chords at the opening of the 'Trio' section were not all accurate. There was not much variety of tone, but a good standard of accuracy generally in notes and rhythm.
STUDY; NO 7 BY CARCASSI—21 out of 24
The tone was uniformly pleasant. Some wrong notes here and there, but it was rhythmical and neat on the whole.
AURAL TESTS;—13 out of 18
Test A2 and B (intervals) were incorrect. Other tests were accurate.
PLAYING AT SIGHT;—16 out of 21
There was some muddled rhythm in this, but a good degree of accuracy in notes.
TOTAL MARKS—123 out of 150. Marks needed to pass—100
GENERAL REMARKS:—*Promising playing, with a nice sense of style.*

Though I was pleased with the results, the classical guitar would always remain a source of secondary importance. Any instrument that demanded attention for eight hours a day sounded like hard work and no play to me; its bastardised descendant would do nicely, thank you. After one particular lesson I called in at the Purple Onion for a sociable coffee. A local Jack the Lad, noticing my guitar, asked what I'd been playing recently.

'Oh, a bit of Fernando Sor,' I replied.

'Is 'e the leather repairer over in Hartlepool?' was the next enquiry.

'No, he was a nineteenth century Spanish composer,' I pointed out.

'Never fuckin' 'eard of 'im. D'ya know any Leapy Lee?' he rounded off. I retired hurt.

I wondered what kind of marking Gladys would have given at a Tramline gig. How about:

'Primitively rhythmic with obvious Long John Baldry-influenced vocals. Musical influence is limited by insistence on the use of repetitive Negro sentiments. The only saving grace is the inclusion of Tansman's 'Mazurka', with its pleasant elementary fusing of native Polish form, inherent with mild bi-tonalism and beset with sure knowledge of the guitar's resources. Shame about the shitty version of that Buffalo Springfield song.'

Island Records press officer Ian Coates had prepared a biography, a copy of which was sent to us. It described us briefly as follows:

"The North East of England has not been notable in the past for producing good R&B bands. The only exception being Newcastle's Animals. Now Teesside has produced a group to rival the famous Tyneside band—TRAMLINE.

Though Tramline has only been together a short while, they have won legions of fans in clubs and colleges, not only around their native Middlesbrough, but also in London. Their music has something of the vitality of the old Animals and Yardbirds, plus their own individual talents".

Short personal statements on each member followed. These snippets of invaluable trivia alerted an unsuspecting public to the fact that John McCoy had "once spent three days driving round London". Yes, that car must have had an exceptionally large petrol tank. Terry Popple's previous endeavours easily belittled that claim to fame as he'd "played in night clubs backing people like Frankie Vaughan, Vince Hill and Elaine Delmar". We also filled out a kind of questionnaire under the heading of Lifelines, though inclusion of it here is mercifully omitted.

August 9-10-11 1968

The 8th National Jazz and Blues Festival. The title was by now slightly misleading due to the rise in popularity of rock music. Supporters of jazz had to settle for a three-and-a-half hour slot on the Saturday afternoon, though I'm sure the assembled talent was satisfactory. For a meagre ten shillings, they could stroke their goatees to the sounds of Jon Hendricks; the Ronnie Scott Quintet; the Don Rendell and Ian Carr Quintet; the Alan Haven Trio and the Mike Westbrook Band. The previous evening, in stark contrast, featured the Herd; the Marmalade; the Taste; Time Box; and from the U.SA.—Jerry Lee Lewis. All for fifteen shillings.

Saturday evening's line up would now be regarded as an almost historical event. The Nice; Jeff Beck; Ten Years After; the Crazy World Of Arthur Brown; Tyrannosaurus Rex (yes, T. Rex); Joe Cocker; the Nite People; Clouds and Deep Purple. Ginger Baker (plus his special guests) took up a 'Special Guest' spot. A month later, *Beat Instrumental* would print the following review:

'Saturday night was opened by the indomitable Joe Cocker, who blasted his way through 'Marjorine', 'With A Little Help From My Friends', and others with great gusto. He was followed by Tyrannosaurus Rex who also got a great reception—especially for 'Deborah', though Marc Bolan's guitar was a bit on the quiet side. The Nice and the Jeff Beck group performed with much volume and intensity, with the former's 'Ars Longa Vita Brevis' creating a good deal of excitement with Roy Harper on tambourine. The Ginger Baker spot, built up as a big surprise, turned out to be Ginger and Phil Seaman on drums with Eric Clapton playing fine guitar—an unusual line-up, but it all worked extremely well. Arthur Brown was beset by almost insuperable problems, but at last he managed to get his circus on parade—jugglers, a girl's choir, a brass band, a fire-eater, belly dancers—forming a fine climax to the evening. From a day that had started off with the Ronnie Scott Quintet, we had indeed gone from the sublime to the ridiculous.

Sadly, I was unable to experience that particular 'experience' due to an engagement at Mothers, Birmingham's home of progressive rock. Our support act, a Teutonic-looking duo with regional accents, made mellow sounds to accompany their thought-provoking lyrics. The audience, sitting cross-legged and attentive, responded in a reciprocal fashion, having 'dug' the set. During the interval, in the exclusive setting of our communal dressing room, one of the Teutonics proffered a rather large roll-up in my direction. I'd avoided any kind of drug up until then, but given the ambience of the evening and the acceptance of the unavoidable, I decided to give it a go. It didn't render me incapable; in fact, I rather enjoyed the set, crossed legs and all, though dismantling the equipment seemed to take ages.

'Come on, I'm waiting to lock up.'

'Yeah, err, right!'

We arrived at Kempton Park with mounting excitement. Traffic jams were a nonentity in Middlesbrough, and my previous trips to London had encountered moving mass rather than static crawl. Still, we managed to gain access to the backstage area in time to witness the start of day three, which featured acts of a more laidback nature to those trying to create an impression on the previous day. There'd be no guitar-slingers comin' home to see their baby in a silver lining on a black night. The same for dagger-wielding organists, ginger drummers and weirdos with their head ablaze. Even ex-gas fitters from Sheffield and dandies who pined for Deborah were passé by now.

This was a day to be cool, man.

Once our van was parked up, I checked out the view from the stage. My initial reaction was akin to that of my first encounter with Ayresome Park, except that the crowd seemed to be sitting on the pitch. And there was a darned sight more of them. Tens of bloody thousands, basking in the sunlight of a glorious summer's day. Thank you, God—and the National Jazz Federation. Entertainment by Eclection, Sonya, the Johnsons, and Al Stewart backed by Fairport Convention were all warmly received, before the Incredible String Band rounded off the afternoon in true hippie fashion, with songs about painting boxes and cosmic journeys. And all for ten shillings. For another fifteen you could witness the evening fare too, though how afternoon-only payees were ejected was a source of interest. Maybe they cleared the whole site and started again.

One and a half hours after the Incredible String Band's conjunction with Gandalf, Tramline struck up with 'Harpoon Man'. To be honest, after an hour of John Peel prattling on about his friend Pig and some unknown bands from Southern California and Cleethorpes, I'd have played a selection of Prussian death marches just to get him off. As a nationally-unknown band, our reception was in keeping with our reputation, which was not enhanced by John McCoy's choice of harmonica for his solo during our slow blues, 'Sorry, Sorry'. The keys of B flat and E have never shared a particularly close musical relationship, especially in front of twenty five thousand people. Chicken Shack would indeed hit the stage at their allocated time.

We hated encores anyway.

Jethro Tull were the sensation of the night, due mainly to Ian Anderson's natural sense of showmanship. He ambled on stage in an ill-fitting overcoat, stood on one leg and played the flute. Say no more. Of course, the accompaniment of messers Abrahams, Cornick and Bunker added the final touches, but make no mistake, Anderson was clearly a star. The ensuing acts, John Mayall, the Spencer Davis Group and Traffic had no chance. Afterwards, I learned that Paul Rodgers had teamed up with Paul Kossoff in a band called Free and were signed to Island Records. The world was indeed a small place. Half of The Road Runners were now recording for the countries hippest label! What next? Dave Usher joining The Stones? Colin Bradley in sex-romp with the Beverly Sisters? In those days, anything could happen.

Back home, my daytime visits to the Purple Onion had found cause for distraction. A girl called Marge had started to attract my attention, due mainly to her detached air and arty look. Eugene, aware of my interest, acted as an intermediary and set the ball rolling.

'Hey, Moody, I'll grab another stool then take it over to her table,' he suggested.

'Then what?' I asked, uncertain of his intentions.

'Then you sit on it,' he replied. So I did.

Marge seemed to be unaware of my position on the local music scene, which, to be honest, posed no problem to my ego. She cited folk clubs as a more natural habitat, though I guessed that her choice of gigs was probably limited by her circle of odd friends. I detected more than a hint of rebellion in this girl, an attribute that appealed to my artistic side. I asked her out and she accepted—it was to be the start of a very long relationship. Soon after, I decided to terminate my weekly visits to Gladys V. Goldsbrough (nee Kirkham) L.R.A.M. A.R.C.M. L.T.C.I.. Segovia could now sleep easy.

At this time, the local rock scene offered little in the way of originality. There was Tramline, Rivers Invitation (a band featuring the remaining members of The Real McCoy), and a handful of semi-pros performing cover versions. All in all, not a great deal to get excited about. Island Records' announcement that 'Somewhere Down the Line' would have a September release placed Tramline torso, body, head and shoulders above the rest. However, my long-term plans included serious thoughts of a permanent move back to London. I had the experience to back it, thank you very much, though the avoidance of Finsbury Park would be part and parcel of any future upheaval. In the meantime, we'd have to make do with an odd mix of one-nighters, which included the Sporting Club at South Bank, an industrial area on the outskirts of Middlesbrough, and home to the then unknown magician Paul Daniels. Incarcerated in the usual weekly cabaret stint was Norman Collier, he of the broken microphone act. A nice chap, he kept us amused in the communal dressing room with a very passable Popeye impersonation before going out to present a well-honed set, temporarily oblivious to the fact that he'd still have to spend at least another four nights in that godforsaken place.

John McCoy's entrepreneurial interests led him into his involvement in the Teespop festival, an adventurous promotion that, to my knowledge, has never been repeated in the Teesside area. Set against a backdrop of industrial pollution, the event featured Traffic, Joe Cocker and the Grease Band and Family. John was involved in the promotion, and local bands, headed by Tramline of course, also had their day. During our spot, I decided to attract some attention by strapping my guitar to my amp stack and turning everything full on. The idea was to create a hail of feedback a la Pete Townshend, though the resulting squeals failed to impress the majority. Further recollections are a distant memory, but I do recall getting pissed on Scotch with David Coverdale and other locals amid the sweet aroma of marijuana, which drifted suspiciously from the direction of Traffic's dressing room.

Family, led by the mercurial partnership of Roger Chapman and Charlie Whitney, refused to appear on the smaller of the two stages and headed off back to London where, no doubt, The Speakeasy beckoned. In fine festival tradition, everything overran and Traffic hit the stage at eleven forty. Twenty-five minutes later, the Police called a halt to the performance, citing midnight as curfew time. In other words—pack up and piss off.

The release of 'Somewhere Down the Line' created little impression. Legendary rhythm and blues pundit Mike Raven played 'Statesboro Blues' on his Sunday evening radio show and was less than enthusiastic. He described our rendition as somewhat inferior to Taj Mahal's version. He was correct. As a teenager with it all before me, I lost little sleep over his critique. This would stand me in good stead for the future—I put it down to experience, then endeavoured to improve by effort. Years later, I added 'and try to keep sober whenever possible.'

If you would hit the mark, you must aim a little above it;
Every arrow that flies feels the attraction of the earth.
                                        Henry Wordsworth Longfellow.

Your first album was crap; this one's much better.
                                        A bloke in a pub.

Somewhere down the line, Tramline ran out of creative fuel and rolled quietly towards the great terminus of failed deliveries. However, we were contracted to make one more album for Island Records. Chris Blackwell, in his wisdom (or possibly wickedness), hired a producer whose reputation did indeed precede him. Guy Stevens had started out as a DJ in the early Sixties, a specialist in soul and R&B, whose influence gave rise to The Who and the Small Faces. His initial involvement with Island was due to his collaboration with Spooky Tooth, though his most successful efforts were with Mott the Hoople. Working with Tramline was purely contractual, though to give him his due, he did his best. In retrospect, I'd say he was as high as a kite on something or other, but his enthusiasm helped us get the best out of our performances:

'Hey man, get a bigger sound on the guitar, that will really make the track rock so the listener will go 'yeah, baby' then wanna hear more and feel good as the drums go badum badum behind the vocals that stretch out over the thud of the bass and Norman can sail like a liner through uncharted seas. Yeah?'

He even came up with the title for the album, the unsurpassed *Moves of Vegetable Centuries*. Spinal Tap would have loved him. Unfortunately, his excessive lifestyle got the better off him and he was dead and buried long before the Tap's rise to infamy.

The recording of *Moves of Vegetables Centuries* was to me, a notable improvement on its predecessor. Once again, we were in and out within a few days, blissfully ignoring the fact that studio technique and a modicum of foresight were required, just to add that extra touch. One lives and learns. Terry Sidgewick had decided to devote more of his time to domestic issues and was replaced by virtuoso bassist Colin Hodgkinson, a move that, to be quite honest, added a real sense of progression. Guy Stevens added his own brand of madness by employing a piano player called Norman, a speed-driven individual who wore a Moss Brothers suit. I'd hazard a guess that he'd come straight off the boats. Unfortunately, his over-enthusiasm resulted in a tendency to play across every bar, space and accent of the music, employing not only both hands, but judging by the end result, both feet as well. Ron Aspery, by then working with the Eric Delaney Band, dropped by with a sax-playing mate to add another dimension to the sound. The end result was a kind of organised jam session, a direction which I felt at ease with; musos enjoying each others company. I doubt if Island Records shared this sentiment as commerciality was seriously overlooked. They did, after all, have a business to run.

ANOTHER BRIEF RETROSPECTIVE CRITIQUE

PEARLY QUEEN—A cover of a Traffic song that had proved to be a showstopper. We'd played it during a gig in Warrington and the promoter came up to the stage and paid us off.

SWEET SATISFACTION—A McCoy–Moody original which was recorded live, with no overdubs. John's lyrical persuasions, though sang in earnest, seemed somewhat unconvincing:
"LIVING IN LOVE NOW, WILL KEEP US TOGETHER, DON'T MIND THE TROUBLE, DON'T MIND THE WEATHER".

Tortured guitar phrases were complemented by Norman's excessive use of Jerry Lee Lewis-style glissandos, which sometimes gave the impression that he was rolling oranges up and down the keyboard.

YOU BETTER RUN—Much better. John's suggestion that we try this Rascals' tune showed good foresight. Ron and his mate joined us on another live take, which features some manic guitar soloing over a driving beat.

GRUNT—Seven minutes and four seconds of instrumental madness, again totally live and unedited. I'd borrowed the main theme from Muddy Waters' 'You Need Love' and suggested a Yardbirds-type rave up as a pointer to the unknown. Popple and Hodgkinson laid down an awesome backing, while the rest of us went… well, mad I suppose. It was great fun at the time..

SWEET MARY—A traditional song that John dedicated to British blues legend Cyril Davies. His heartfelt vocal performance was enhanced by some wonderful alto sax soloing from Ron, who together with his nameless friend, were now enjoying the benefits of the small keg of cider that they'd installed in their sound booth. An overdub was administered by me in the shape of an open-tuned slide solo. Norman managed to suppress the glissandos until the beginning of the fade. Shame

I WISH YOU WOULD—More mania-instilled playing on this Billy Boy Arnold favourite. Totally live with some nice dynamics around the halfway mark. Rock-steady drumming from Terry and the usual glissandos from you-know-who towards the end.

GOOD MORNING LITTLE SCHOOLGIRL—An authentic sounding interpretation of the Sonny Boy Williamson song which featured just John, Norman and myself. Norman excelled, ignored any use of the dreaded glissando and provided a respectable accompaniment to my Hubert Sumlin impersonation, which I performed sans plectrum. Overdubbed harmonica.

HARRIET'S UNDERGROUND RAILWAY—Another McCoy–Moody composition that was written on the spot. The title was provided by Ron and had very little to do with the lyrical content, which dealt with adverse feelings and instability:

"I'M TIRED OF THIS CONFUSION, BREAKING UP LIKE CRYSTAL IN MY MIND" etc. Nevertheless, the backing was pretty funky, chugging along to an exquisite bass line and without the aid of overdubs. Island Records may well have proffered another frugal sum in advance of future earnings. This would, no doubt, have resulted in a quick visit to Take 6.

A letter from Bruce Thomas appeared in the November edition of *Beat Instrumental* under a heading entitled 'Sustain'. It acknowledged the number of letters received from frustrated blues guitarists with finger vibrato problems, and set out to ease their worried minds. He explained that the fingering technique employed by Beck, Clapton, Hendrix etc, was slightly different to that used by classical players. These differences were then fully described over a number of paragraphs, culminating in the, for some, enlightening news that the vibrato could be employed whilst the note was being "bent up a semitone as in blues playing."

Now, there's a man with too much spare time on his hands, I thought.

I tried to imagine what spare time looked like on ones' hands. Did it feel like hessian, or glow at night? What colour was it? I knew people who'd never done a day's work in their lives. Their hands must have been covered in it.

There was no ill-feeling or resentment regarding the demise of Tramline. We'd given it a shot and had enjoyed our time together, but it was time to move on. John had his business interests and Terry Popple and myself wanted to see a bit of the world, which in the Sixties was par for the course. We even went out on a positive note. Disc and Music Echo's November 23rd edition ran an article on the British blues scene that praised the up and coming names. "...Savoy Brown Blues Band, Black Cat Bones, Dr. K's Blues Band, Duster Bennet, Love Sculpture, Tramline, Taste, Led Zeppelin, Free, Bakerloo Line...the list is virtually endless and all are good, solid blues groups, each with that essential ingredient of musical honesty". Praise indeed for an obsolete act. The preceding page ran a half page advertisement from Island Records in conjunction with One Stop Record Shops. Minimalist in its approach, it read: Fairport Convention—Traffic—Spooky Tooth—Tramline—Jethro Tull. We were up there with the big boys but it was too late. Pity. The remaining weeks of 1968 served as a period of introspection, a breathing space that saw my relationship with Marge blossom into a full-time commitment. Together with Terry and his girlfriend, B, we greeted the New Year resplendent in fancy dress at the Kirk, where resolutions had somewhat more than a sense of frivolity about them. It was time to move on.

A Cold Sweat in Wood Green

Resolutions were for the half-hearted, the weak and the middle-aged, and in my opinion, surplus to requirement for ambitious teenagers. Anyway, a famous music journal was about to play its part in my future plans. In January 1969, I required no encouragement whatsoever to scan the *Melody Maker*'s 'Musicians Wanted' section—the country's premier job centre for professional and semi-professional performers. For a shilling a word, anybody could lure the aforementioned into a world of the unknown, the untried, or the totally uncalled for. Caution would always be the key word. If, for instance, the one-lined small print read: Guitarist wanted for three month stint in Turkish bar, apply to Flat 27, 39 Squalid Road, Limehouse, London E.14., scepticism would be advisable. Alternatively, a bold-printed box advertisement offering a singer the pole-position with a top twenty band that guaranteed fame, fortune and a regular supply of groupies, would be hard to ignore. Lady Luck would hold the key to my destiny.

Lucas and the Mike Cotton Sound were an established soul band who worked most nights of the week on the club/college circuit. My common denominator with this outfit was two-fold:

1) they were represented by Cana Variety (refer to The Wildflowers) and

2) Tramline had played support during a gig at Chelsea College of Art, where John McCoy, as a previous promoter at Kirklevington, had introduced me to the respected bandleader.

Mike was, and still is, an amiable guy and a true pro. Our meeting would stand me in good stead as an interested party for his *Melody Maker* advertisement early in January:

GUITARIST REQUIRED
FOR TOP SOUL BAND
TEL: Mayfair 1436

I recognised the number instantly, but lacked the confidence to pick up a telephone and put myself in the frame. Silly really, considering that my guitar playing was known to both bandleader and agent. Once again, John acted on my behalf and announced an audition at the Fishmongers Arms, Wood Green the following week. My lack of self-assurance would, I felt sure, be rectified by my nimble fingers. Having spent numerous evenings at his clubs over the years, listening to the sounds of local DJ Tony Hargan, I was pretty au fait with soul and Tamla Motown music, plus I'd already seen Lucas, Mike and the boys in action. However, where there's an audition, there's competition.

The Fishmongers Arms was no different to hundreds of late Victorian or early Edwardian public houses spread out across London, apart from the added attraction of a banqueting suite, or in this case, a 'back room'. As a gig, it had been an established venue for jazz before giving way to blues, soul, and rock. The relatively short tube journey from Kings Cross brought back memories of 1967, especially when we passed through Finsbury Park. I wondered if Dilip Chowdhury (LDS RCS) was somewhere up above me, administering his own unique brand of metallurgy on some unsuspecting soul. Instinctively, I felt my own front teeth, briefly mourned the loss of the originals, then shook my head in disbelief. An Indonesian nurse sitting opposite observed this impromptu reaction and shifted uneasily in her seat. I left the train wearing a tight-lipped expression and contemplated an afternoon of ventriloquism. Before entering the pub, I made a mental note to avoid asking for a bottle of beer. Once inside, I espied Mike Cotton and a couple of the band at the bar (where else?), and after brief introductions, we made our way to the small hall where I encountered my rivals.

David O'List had made a name for himself as the guitarist with the original Nice line-up, though it had soon become apparent that the awesome talents of organist Keith Emerson expressed little mercy for stragglers. He appeared nervous and unsure of himself. Recent press reports had stated that he was now a member of a new outfit called Roxy Music, so I was quite surprised to see him at the audition. A quick mental deduction suggested that he'd been relieved of his duties. The third and final competitor was a nerdy-looking individual called Jim Roach, who'd played in the original line-up of John Hiseman's Colosseum. He was obviously a good player, but his ability to soul-stir seemed suspect. I weighed up the odds and concluded that a move to London was on the cards. In the meantime, the provisions were on the table and the pudding was ready for the tastebud test.

Sensitive to O'List's unease, Mike decided to alleviate the poor lad's apprehension by allowing him to bat first, leaving Jim Roach and myself obliged to avoid eye contact. Lucas, the band's singer and showman entered at this moment amid wafts of after shave, offered a raised palm and requested 'Gimme five!' from anybody in close proximity. The reciprocal slaps, infused with enthusiasm, resounded throughout the empty hall like circus sea lions vying for fish. A real character, Lucas was the genuine article as far as soul singers went. An African-American by birth, Bruce McPherson Lucas had moved from his native Ohio courtesy of Uncle Sam's draft board to serve time in England, before settling down with a local lass to start a family. I was later informed that this union had produced two fine sons, Otis and Marvin, but being young, gullible and prime fodder for piss-takers, I remained somewhat unconvinced.

The band's choice of audition material centred mainly around standard soul hits like 'Cold Sweat' and 'Dance to the Music', which required a disciplined rhythmic approach. Poor old David just didn't seem to be on the same wavelength or, for that matter, the same planet, even though he made an effort to look presentable by wearing a nice white shirt. His Wah Wah-induced raga variations were an unfortunate choice that lent nothing to the melodies and grooves peculiar to James Brown or Sly and the Family Stone. Consequently, the lad was sent for an early bath after two songs. Jim went next into the fray and did well, but confidence in my ability to impress remained undaunted. I did my bit and was voted in on a five to one decision. The drummer preferred Mr Roach whom it later transpired was slightly miffed by the result. Still, he did gain respect a few years later as a player on the jazz-fusion scene. David O'List accepted the decision with dignity, though his progress has eluded me ever since. You win some, you lose some.

Things was clicking for me, man—Muddy Waters.

Confidence in one's ability is a credible attribute. However, the conse-quences must, by the same token, be taken into consideration. I had no hesitation in moving my girlfriend, my equipment and my meagre belong-ings to a new destination and more importantly, a new life. Marge had no particular longing to remain in Middlesbrough, and the chance to move on was too good to pass by. The fact that my new-found employment required almost immediate participation, meant relocation was sudden. Parents and loved ones were somewhat taken by surprise, but through a haze of concern, a ray of optimism shone. I think they appreciated that, though we were only eighteen, our minds were made up. Furthermore, setting aside the insecurities of self-employment, I'd been promised a decent weekly wage. Who cares about money at that age anyway? We didn't. However, we did require a bit of a kick-start.

Martin was an Australian hippie who had it well sussed. He'd landed a job where he could wear his hair half-way down his back, dress scruff-ily and indulge in a, near as damn it, rock and roll lifestyle. He wasn't a musician, he was the next best thing—a roadie. I had no idea as to how long he'd been employed by Lucas and the Mike Cotton Sound, but the fact that he referred to his masters as 'Lurid and the Quite Rotten Sound' indicated a certain air of familiarity. He lived in a bedsit in large semi-detached house in Hornsey, north London, a pleasant area near, surprise surprise, Finsbury Park! Luck had it my teeth were behaving themselves, so dental paranoia remained in check. The luck continued as Martin informed us that a room in the same building was available for occupancy the following week, and were we interested. If so, we could sleep on his floor until we received the keys to our independence. Yes! And my first gig as a Mike Cotton man was in two days time.

Memo: Have entered the fast lane—buy a diary and some 'Lime Essence' Old Spice.

Life in the conventional lanes for Lucas and the Mike Cotton Sound was undertaken by two particular modes of transport, namely a Ford Zephyr six car and a Commer van. As the band's line-up consisted of tenor sax, trumpet, trombone, bass, drums, guitar and Lucas, two of the members were usually required to accompany Martin and the equipment. To my recollection, there was some kind of rota system employed to keep everyone happy, though whoever adopted the 'middle-man' position in the Commer had drawn the short straw. The location of the vehicle's engine between the driver and passenger seats meant the unlucky one was required to perch on its plastic casing for the duration. This could be uncomfortable and somewhat warm around the nether regions, but we never really complained. These guys were real pros and I was pleased to be amongst them. Soon, I would begin to understand what being 'on the road' was all about.

Mike Cotton had gained a very credible reputation as the youngest bandleader on the early Sixties 'trad' band scene, fronting his Jazzmen on trumpet and spiel. Trombonist John 'Jazzboat' Beecham had accompanied Mike during his metamorphism to the Mike Cotton Sound, a unit that stayed abreast of the current musical trends. Lucas, a showman of the first order, sang sweet soul music and could dance like a man possessed. On saxophone and flute was Nick Newell, whom I recognised from the classic Zoot Money's Big Roll Band. The rhythm section was made up of drummer Bernie Higgins (nee Higginson), who was known affectionately as Shillin'. This was due to his occasionally unkempt appearance, as in "lend us a shillin' for a cup of tea, mate". Jim Rodford complemented the line-up on bass. They'd featured a keyboard player once, a guy called Dave Rowberry, who went on to take over Alan Price's job in the Animals and wasn't replaced. It would have necessitated a bigger car anyway.

Twenty Four Hours From Tulse Hill

Typical Set-list—january 1969.
Soul Serenade
Spinning Wheel
House Of The Rising Sun
Big Bird
Harlem Shuffle
Dance To The Music
Cold Sweat
Hey Dude
Shake A Tail Feather
Don't Fight It
Lucas' Dance Spot, Featuring: Ride Your Pony, The Mashed Potato And
Land Of A Thousand Dances
It's Your Thing
More Of The Same.............

The club scene was thriving and the band had built up a pretty good fan-base over the years and worked most days of the week to good houses. Being a video, internet-free era, young people had little to distract them from basic, down-the-line entertainment. Today's comprehensive choice of strong lagers and alco-pops were preceded by rather weaker pints of bitter and single-measure gin and orange squash. If you wanted to get drunk quickly, there was always Carlsberg Special Brew and Barley Wine. Meanwhile in America, somebody called Richard Nixon was inaugurated as President. He preferred bourbon (quite a lot of it, apparently).

Lucas' stage wear was something else. He wore two-piece satin suits of which he had three; red, gold and silver. Their appearance would be best described as garish. To complement these spectacular creations, he chose a pair of Chelsea boots. Though they'd walked off the cobbler's bench a dark shade of brown, they were soon rendered chalky white by their new owner, whose prowess with a brush and a tin of emulsion paint was, to be honest, limited. This tasteless trio travelled the land in a homemade carrying bag, which had eventually earned itself the title of "the body". I never did manage to discover the travelling arrangements for the boots, but they turned up at every gig—literally. Prior to every performance, Lucas would spend a considerable amount of time arranging his processed hair into a splendid pompadour, which was then kept in-situ with a small silk scarf or 'do-rag'. This little act of ritualistic vanity proved to be counter-productive, for as soon as he let out his first James Brown-inspired 'Oowwww!', the whole structure collapsed into an untidy plumage, which required constant attention.

Once, after a show in Bristol, we all went for a drink at the Granary Club, where a local soul band were just finishing their first set. Lucas got chatting to the singer at the bar and was invited to get up and sing a song in the second set. He agreed, providing he could take yours truly with him. When the band announced their special guest, he turned to me: 'OK—'Stand By Me' in C'. As soon as I strapped on the guitar, I turned to the rest of the band with a mischievous grin and whispered: 'Stand by Me—in E flat!' After a quick once round the chord-sequence, Lucas came in: 'When the...When the night...When the...he glanced towards me for help. I shook my head in a way that laid all blame on the poor unsuspecting band, leaving Lucas to plough through the rest of the song in an assortment of unexpected keys.

Another aspect of the one-nighter scene was the hotel situation. My previous experiences bade no more than bed and breakfast holidays in Blackpool and Scarborough, a week in Lourdes, Mrs Mcbean's home from home, and the odd four-to-a-room bunk-up with Tramline. Now I could experience the glamour of the two- and even three-star abodes peculiar to travelling salesmen and the like. Night porters, usually called Tom or Bill, could be roused from their slumbers by requests for sustenance and beverage ('Ham or cheese, bottled beer only'). One old boy, who looked dead to the world, denied that he'd been sleeping at all, merely "Taking a good look at the inside of my eyelids". Yeah, sure.

Within a month of joining the band I was taking part in one of those now-legendary Sixties package tours backing Gene Pitney, gracing the stages of some of the most prestigious venues in the country. Gene Pitney had always been, well, Gene Pitney. I was familiar with his hits, which were often dramatic semi-dirges about hurt, and heartache. Even the odd sprightly tune somehow sounded somewhat ominous. However, he still commanded respect as a serious professional performer and attracted large audiences. The work schedule looked impressive; three and a half weeks of cinemas/ theatres (two shows a night), plus two weeks of cabaret. I turned to Jim Rodford for reassurance.

'What's Gene Pitney like then?'

'What Old Squeaky? He's alright, and if you stand behind him on stage when he's in the spotlight, you can count the veins in his sticky-out ears!'

Jim was as nice a guy as you could get. It was a pity that the tour would be his swansong with the band. He'd already started rehearsing with Rod Argent, Russ Ballard and Bob Henrit in what was to become the very successful Argent. The only redeeming aspect to his departure was that Rod Argent provided the necessary keyboard parts for the Pitney tour.

As it turned out, Gene was all right, if a little on the intense side. He'd been using the band on his annual tour for a number of years, so rehearsals consisted of a couple of days at the good old Fishmongers Arms, to brush up on the old material. We also learned his most recent offering, which had failed—so far—to make an impression on the charts. However, he was, as I would soon realise, a very popular live attraction. He was accompanied at all times by his personal assistant-come-minder, a rather large chap called Malcolm Cook, and quite often by Ron King, tour manager and representative of the Arthur Howes booking agency. He arrived, rehearsed and left. No pints in the pub with the lads afterwards. It was all very professional, and you couldn't knock it. After the rehearsal we all trooped over to the BBC Television Centre and recorded a half hour show for BBC Two's *Colour Me Pop*, which was screened the following Saturday. 'I'm on the telly, Mam!'

Colour Me Pop was the forerunner to *Disco 2*, which in turn became the hugely successful the *Old Grey Whistle Test*. Originally broadcast in black and white, it was inaugurated in colour only a year or so before— hence the title. It was my first time in a TV studio and it felt rather strange performing to cameramen and technicians, some with clipboards. A few years later I recorded *Disco 2* with Juicy Lucy, then *OGWT* with Snafu. The only difference was that Pitney's show was live, whereas the others were mimed to playback. And you received a free badge from the Whistle Test. Even later, when I played the *OGWT* with Whitesnake, we performed live in a much bigger studio. I assume the size of the studio was commensurate with the amount of volume the bands pumped out. We never had that problem with Gene!

The line-up for the Gene Pitney tour was interesting. Lucas and The Mike Cotton Sound opened the show with three songs, followed by compere Mike Quinn, who introduced The Iveys, a new signing for the Beatles' company, Apple. They would later evolve into Badfinger, a band destined for tragedy a few years later, when two of the guys committed suicide within a month of each other. After their set, the smartly groomed compère held the audience's attention whilst equipment was jostled into place. I didn't envy the imperturbable Mr Quinn his job. You're only there as a distraction; and you're on you own. It must have been lonely out there, especially in Glasgow and Liverpool. Joe Cocker and the Grease Band closed the first set, much to my delight. Tramline had supported them a couple of times, which had given me the opportunity to get to know the guys and I dug their music. Their guitarist, an amiable Irishman named Henry McCulloch, had a lovely, lazy style and a warm tone that seemed to reflect his personality. Also, they gave a whole new meaning to the word stoned. What a bunch! After their set they'd glide back to the dressing room for more spliffs.

Following the interval, we did a couple more, Mike Quinn entertained/suffered, then Marmalade took to the stage. Their performances were always very slick and professional, and featured a left-handed guitarist, Junior Campbell, who played in a right-handed fashion whilst tuned to the chord of E major—very odd. Once finished, they would disappear backstage and beyond with a bevy of groupies. Well, according to drummer Alan Whitehead's *News of the World* expose a couple of years later, they did. I was too busy doing three sets, twice a night to notice. Yes, two shows a night, and usually sold out. Time for the build-up, Mr Quinn.

I tell you, this guy Pitney was popular. Lots of women and quite a bit of screaming! I'd never experienced this kind of reception before. Alright, I know it wasn't directed at me personally, but I was standing pretty close to the object of their arousal, and it was exciting (no, not standing close to Gene Pitney—the noise they were making!). It must have had something to do with his heartfelt delivery, pained expression and helpless vulnerability, because he wasn't exactly predominant in the hunky looks department. Some fans even threw small toys and trinkets onto the stage. One or two threw themselves.

As the *Melody Maker* review for the first show stated: "You have to hand it to Gene Pitney. This young man with a neat, short hairstyle and wearing a smart blue suit with collar and tie has the magnetism of any of the more fashionable longhaired pop stars. Here he is on yet another British tour, still packing 'em in and managing to evoke the screams. But he keeps them in good order and the dozen or so stewards on hand at the opening show at the Odeon Birmingham were not really needed."

They'd probably have been of more use rounding up Marmalade's groupies, or as a relay team providing round the clock supplies of Rizla papers for Joe Cocker and the Grease Band.

Joe and his band had obviously been booked onto the tour on the strength of their recent number one hit, 'A Little Help From My Friends'. Well, obvious to everyone except them. They didn't include it in their act! Instead, they performed songs like Bob Dylan's 'I Shall Be Released', Jose Feliciano's 'Hitchcock Railway', and a funky rendition of 'Lawdy Miss Clawdy'. Promoter Arthur Howes was not impressed. Neither was the audience, who weren't exactly the Woodstock crowd that Joe would soon be wowing. I can only assume that Mr Howes got his point across as 'Little Help' eventually appeared in the set. Marmalade had no qualms about performing their recent number one, a cover of the Beatles' 'Ob-La-Di, Ob-La-Da', and of course it went down a bomb. I hated it—give me 'Hitchcock Railway' any day.

By the third or fourth gig, I'd formed the impression that Pitney was being somewhat safeguarded from Cocker's crowd. This was confirmed when keyboard player Chris Stainton, strategically placed for the star's arrival, shouted out 'Hi Gene', in a way which suggested 'hygiene'. Gene's assistant Malcolm Cook, sensing dissension in the ranks, immediately bundled his perplexed employer into his dressing room, and slammed the door. Stainton, sporting a slightly sardonic smile, headed back to Cockerville.

Joe Cocker and The Grease Band weren't the only ones smoking the old weed. The Iveys were partial to the odd spliff too, and on some of the longer coach journeys I accepted the odd one myself (just to be sociable, of course). This respect for social graces almost got the better of me a few nights later when I had a blast of a joint before taking to the stage for Pitney's set. As we started the intro for 'Twenty Four Hours from Tulsa', I suddenly became aware of hundreds of people staring at ME! And why did everything seem so detached and slow moving? My onset of paranoia was only momentarily disturbed, as Gene Pitney's entrance distracted the eyes of the masses, and I was left to hyperventilate in peace. Well not quite. Due to an ever-mounting state of panic, I began to shake. Now, shaking is never advisable when playing guitar, especially when performing before a big crowd, because the involuntary movements, in this case coupled with a sudden introduction of perspiration, can encourage one to hit the wrong notes. My instinct for survival prompted me to keep the volume control on my guitar set to very low. By the second tune I was almost inaudible. Luckily, Pitney's crowd was usually littered with a few screamers, which helped. Rod Argent gave me what was, to all intents and purposes, a friendly smile, but his expression suddenly took on the leer of a character from a painting by Hieronymus Bosch. Shit! What was happening?

Gene, aware that something was slightly amiss in the guitar section, shot me the odd glance, which, I reassured myself, was better than being shot by the odd gun. I managed to hang on, and by the fifth song the effects were starting to wear off, encouraging the colour to return to my cheeks. After the show, nobody said a word about my curiously introvert performance, suggesting that they were either very understanding or just as stoned as I was. In Gene's case, I'm sure he'd put it down to stage fright.

February's *Beat Instrumental* ran a feature headed 'Stateside Report,' and praised the talents of Pogo, "an impressive quintet headed by guitarists Richie Furay and Jim Messina". I'm sure that the members of Poco were suitably bewildered by this newly chosen title. Also, according to B.I.'s reliable sources, Steve Stills' new band featuring David Crosby and Graham Nash may be called Frozen Noses. Nudge, nudge, say no more. Under a sub-heading, we were also informed that Mike Bloomfield had changed his name to Makel Blumfeld, and together with Barry Goldberg had produced an album called 'Two Jews' Blues'. Van Morrison was referred to as 'the old vocalist with Them', and Mason Williams had recorded an album with the thought-provoking title, 'The Mason Williams Ear Show'.

As I said earlier, the Sixties had a lot to answer for.

Tuning into the radio guaranteed the listener some great soul music. In the Top Twenty at the time was Diana Ross and the Supremes, and the Temptations performing 'I'm Gonna Make You Love Me', 'Dancing in the Street' by Martha and the Vandellas, 'For Once In My Life' by Stevie

Wonder, 'Private Number' by Judy Clay and William Bell, 'I Guess I'll Always Love You' by the Isley Brothers, 'I'll Pick A Rose For My Rose' (or as I used to sing, 'I'll pick my nose for our Rose') by Merv Johnson, 'People' by the Tymes and 'Stop Her on Sight (SOS)' by Edwin Starr.

Inspirational guitar was provided by Fleetwood Mac with 'Albatross', Peter Green's beautiful yet melancholic air. I missed playing blues, and as a member of Lucas and the Mike Cotton Sound, it was soul music all the way. Killing time in dressing rooms gave me the opportunity to bend the blue notes in a self-satisfying manner, but once on stage it was mostly RHYTHM! And, to be honest, it was fun. Get on up, baby!

The Pitney tour gave me a personal insight into the well-oiled mechanism that is the pop world. Though Lucas and the Mike Cotton Sound were, in theory, bottom of the bill, we were also backing the star turn, and therefore in a prime position to observe the day-to-day lives of people in the public eye. Alongside Joe Cocker and the lads with their joints, and Marmalade's licentious behaviour, it almost cried out for squeaky-clean Gene to blow his image and do something really outrageous. Alas, it was not to be. Well, not quite. Apparently, Gene and his wife had flown into London a couple of days before the start of the tour, intending to visit Harrods and exclusive clothes shops in the Bond Street area. As they checked in to Pitney's usual hotel, The Westbury, the head receptionist welcomed him warmly. 'Ah, Mr Pitney, so good to see you again. Would you and your wife like the same suite you had last year.' A commendable suggestion, had Mrs Pitney been party to the previous year's arrangement. She wasn't, allegedly.

On another occasion, Cocker and his band had procured a rather large amount of marijuana, which was wrapped up in a sheet of newspaper like fish and chips. Within minutes of arriving at their dressing room, the first of what was to be many joints was being rolled. Meanwhile, in the room next door, Marmalade took to throwing handfuls of their publicity photos out of the window to fans and autograph hunters below. It was a gesture appreciated by everyone except a couple of local cops, who regarded it, somewhat impetuously, as an irresponsible act. Their immediate reaction was to dash upstairs, burst into the dressing room, then admonish the perpetrators for their reckless behaviour. This little manoeuvre was carried out with flawless professionalism. However, they fell at the last hurdle and entered Cocker's room by mistake. 'Right, whoever's chuckin' photos out the window, pack it in, now!' commanded the taller of the two. Through a haze of sweet-smelling smoke, a bunch of guys froze, hearts beating hard, paranoia building up inside. They could already see the headlines in the following morning's papers.

POP STARS IN DRUG BUST.
HEMP SMOKERS CAUGHT IN THE ACT.
LIVERPOOL EMPIRE SHAMED BY HASH-HEADS.

The room became deathly quiet as the guilty-faced deviants awaited their fate. You could have heard a cigarette paper drop.

'I don't care who you are, one more photograph through that window and you'll be arrested!' warned the fatter one. Then, giving the stunned 'heads' a stern look, they left, slamming the door behind them. There were some very relieved men in that room. I know—I was one of them.

While I was away, Marge managed to find us a flat in... guess where? Yes—Finsbury Park! This had to be more than a coincidence. It didn't really matter though; at least we could call it our own. The tour rolled on for almost a month before the final performance at the Blackpool ABC. To most of the performers it was just another gig in another town, but to Joe Cocker and the Grease Band it was regarded as the final hours before liberation from artistic internment—and they'd resolved to make the most of it. It was plainly obvious when they all fell through the stage door that they hadn't spent the afternoon on the Golden Mile. They were drunk as well as stoned, and much rowdier than usual. Bassist Alan Spenner looked as though he'd spent the previous night abusing members of the Rat Pack, whilst guitarist Henry McCullogh seemed to be sporting a pair of strawberry-tinted monocles. Closer inspection revealed them to be his eyes. That night they gave what can loosely be described as a tumultuous performance.

As they stumbled onto the stage, it was immediately obvious that Cocker, Stainton and drummer Bruce Rowlands were merely out of it, whereas Spenner and McCullogh were flying dangerously close to the point of no return. Spenner wore nothing but a bath towel, an unusual choice for a rock performer, but most disturbingly and with the aid of Sellotape, he'd managed to distort his face to take on the look of Charles Laughton's Quasimodo on mescaline. It was a hideous image that disturbed many in the audience. The rest were merely bemused. During the second number Henry McCullogh fell flat on his face and somehow managed to break four strings on his guitar. As he wasn't carrying a spare, this presented a bit of a problem. He looked around for help and saw me in the wings.

'Have you seen help?' he enquired in desperation.

'No, but I've got a Telecaster you can borrow,' I replied sympathetically. He smiled as he collided with his amplifier.

Luckily, my 'Tele' was already old and somewhat scratched because it took a couple of knocks in the remaining songs. I got it back after their set minus the volume control, which was later retrieved. Promoter Arthur Howes witnessed the performance and vowed that the band would never work that circuit again. They were extremely happy with his decision.

During the tour, Lucas had the easiest job of all, which was to sing two songs at the beginning of the show. After that, his time was his own. I'd often see him back at the hotel, happily ensconced at the bar in the company of a lonely travelling salesman, partaking in what was known as the 'Lucas blag'. This consisted of an extremely street-wise American soul singer who wanted to get pissed, and a relatively naïve individual with a bar tab. Lucas could charm the hind legs off the proverbial donkey, which he did with alarming consistency. Many's the time we'd enter the bar to the strains of 'No, no Lucas, I'll get this round—tell us some more stories!' Once the rest of the band joined in, the poor sod would either fade into the background or eventually fall of his stool. We liked to think that it brightened up their day, or in the case of the hotel bible salesmen, the will to carry on living.

After the Pitney theatre tour, we had a week or so before we met up with him again. Cana had thoughtfully filled this period with a handful of gigs. Unfortunately, their thoughts must have wandered at some point, because a date in Newcastle was followed the next day by a gig somewhere in Somerset. Along with Jim Rodford, I found myself assigned to van duty, so we left earlier than the others, in order that Martin could unload and set up the equipment. Heading south down the A1, we passed the infamous Scotch Corner Hotel where, a few years earlier, a couple of the Rolling Stones had been done for urinating against a garage wall. Shameful behaviour. We'd travelled a couple of hundred yards further when Martin realised that we were almost running on empty. Unsure of reaching the next filling station in time, he decided to turn round and head back to Scotch Corner to fill up, and maybe have a piss in honour of the Stones.

The A1 was a busy road, but U-turns were still allowed at allocated spots, if you were in the outside lane. Martin slowed down and proceeded to turn into the gap in the central reservation, when we suddenly felt a bump at the rear of the van. The van seemed to lean to the right, and a second or two later we were on two wheels, looking at the world outside from a different angle. What made the whole thing so strange was that it all seemed to happen in slow motion. We were looking at each other with the most surprised expressions; the look that says, 'What the fuck's going on?' Bits of debris and dust that you wouldn't normally notice was flying around our heads as the vehicle surrendered to the laws of gravity. After what seemed like an eternity, the van, with its occupants and load, came to rest on its side in the middle of the A1 (southbound).

It's true what people say about the immediate aftermath of an accident; that initial period of confused calmness when your brain tries to access the situation. In our case it may have been:

MARTIN THE ROADIE: I'm lying on my side, against the window, with Rodford and Moody on top of me. Must get out.

JIM RODFORD: I'm in a horizontal position in an upturned van, sandwiched between two people who may well start to panic in a few seconds. Come to think of it, so might I.

ME: Well, it could be worse. At least nobody's lying on top of me. Hold on, I think I'm starting to paniiiiiic!

Being the nearest to a door that wasn't touching asphalt, it was up to me to reach for the handle, which I did. Once the door was open, I scrambled out, using Jim and Martin as stepping stones. Sorry lads, but I was panicking, remember? And anyway, I weighed less than nine-and-a-half stone in those days. If Demis Roussos had been the guitarist, they'd never have got out alive.

The guy who'd caused the accident was most apologetic, and rightly so. He said he hadn't realised we were turning, which resulted in him clipping our rear inside at just the right angle to turn us on our side. In other words, he wasn't looking were he was going. Maybe he was discussing the high cost of third-party car insurance with his wife. Well, if he wasn't, he soon would be. The police arrived, took statements, then called for a breakdown truck. Before we could get the van back into position, we had to unload all the equipment onto the central reservation. Once the vehicle was righted, we loaded it all back in. Incredibly, there seemed to be little noticeable damage. Oh, and we were alright too.

The van was in relatively good shape considering what it had just been through. We'd lost Martin's window and wing mirror, one of the doors was held together with string, and a panel-beater would be required at some point. But the thing still went, and so did we—to the gig in Somerset. Intrepid troupers we were, but it was bloody cold outside, and just as cold inside without the full compliment of windows. We stopped en route for something to eat, and for a laugh I bought a roll of bandage and some tomato ketchup. When we finally arrived at the venue, I wrapped the bandage round my head, then added a couple of circles of ketchup to create the illusion that I'd had a nasty bump. It worked! On stage, the rest of the band was doing their best, using the support band's equipment. And their guitarist and bass player were helping out as best they could, though not necessarily in the same key. We were greeted like long lost friends, especially yours truly who, greatly hindered by a seemingly serious head injury, soldiered on till the end. Joe Bradley's words rang loud and clear: "It's all part of your education!" So was appearing in cabaret.

Where's There's Muck, There's More Muck

The North East was rife with cabaret clubs, and I'd prided myself on managing to avoid them. However, at the end of the theatre tour, Gene was booked to appear for a week at the Showboat in my hometown of Middlesbrough, followed by a week at the world famous Batley Variety Club in South Yorkshire. The former, once the Astoria ballroom where I'd both seen the Beatles and performed with the Road Runners, had now been transformed into a top class nightclub. To my advantage, backing Gene Pitney at the Showboat gained a bit more street-cred than standing behind Al Cortina at the Contessa Club.

'Oy, can ya tone it down, I can't 'ear meself arguing with the wife!'

They also had a better class of bouncer. Today, if you look at bouncers—or should I say doormen—they're more often than not, big shaven-headed things in Godfather-style overcoats. In 1969 at the Showboat, they were invariably white, smart-suited, overweight, and for the most part, looking like they'd just come from a Ku Klux Klan meeting in Alabama. One in particular had the kind of stomach that suggested he'd been force-fed cement. They all seemed to drink and smoke, and were past masters at avoiding any sort of exercise, though my judgement may be a little unfair. Let's just say 99.9% of them. On a rowdy night they were told to throw people out; on a quiet night they were told to throw people in.

Pitney was obviously big in Middlesbrough and we played to packed houses every night. I recognised some members of the audience, and it was strange to see them out of their work clothes, so well-scrubbed and dapper-looking. The steelworks were still active which guaranteed not only a high turnout, but also fantastic sales for chicken-in-a-basket table meals. One of the backstage crew told me that one guy, still ravenous after the chicken and chips, actually ate the basket as well, while another guy, a huge docker, ate part of a table! There again, I was only eighteen, and they do take the piss up there.

Now that Jim and Rod had left to concentrate on Argent, Lem Lubin joined as a permanent replacement on bass, and an overweight John Steed look-alike called Peter was taken on as pianist for the two weeks of cabaret. Lem had been the guitarist with Unit 4 plus 2, and was part of the Hertfordshire musical mafia that included Jim, Rod, Russ Ballard and Bob Henrit. Yes, it's an incestuous business! Peter the pianist was an archetypal session musician of the old school, which meant he could read fly shit and always performed in an evening suit. On stage he stood out like a sore thumb against our all-black and chiffon scarf creations. And he was old enough to be my dad! He also found it difficult to hang on to his money, losing most of it in the casino over the duration. If Lemmy from Motörhead acquired his assumed title due to repeated requests to "Lemmy a quid 'till Friday", then Peter the pianist should have been re-christened Ernie as in "Ernie chance of a sub?" Poor old sod.

Gene changed things a bit for the cabaret set. For a start it was longer, which meant learning a couple of new, or should I say old, songs, includ-ing 'Scarlet Ribbons', in which the star attempted to accompany himself on acoustic guitar. Responsibility for tuning the acoustic before each gig was given to me. As soon as I picked it up I had an almost overwhelm-ing urge to take it to the nearest charity shop. The strings were so old they were more thatched than wound, and no matter how hard I tried I just couldn't get the thing in tune. After the first show, Gene complained about the tuning. I stressed that if a guitar were technically out of tune with itself, it would be out of tune with everything else (including his own voice, which had acquired a sudden sharpness on particularly high notes). He gave me a quizzical look before handing the instrument to Malcolm Cook, who conveyed a similar glance in my direction. New strings were purchased and fitted, which helped a little, but at the end of the day, you can't get it right with shite.

During our run at the Showboat my dad came to see the show. He was probably a bit out of his depth in a nightclub, but he didn't show it. At the bar, I introduced him to Lucas and they got on like a house on fire. It was nice of Lucas to make a fuss of him, and I think he even bought Dad a drink! I honestly don't know what they talked about or what common ground they shared, though I'm sure that I figured in their conversation. Maybe they were discussing my individual dress code that consisted of a brown jacket with yellow candy-stripes (blagged from Tom Evans of the Iveys), black crushed-velvet trousers, a mauve 'granddad' tee-shirt, a Rupert the Bear scarf and blood-red monkey boots. If they weren't, I'm sure other people were; I did look slightly out of place.

'That lad looks like a bloody painting box!'

'He must be with the 'Turn'.

'I 'ope Gene bloody Pitney's not like that!' Two chances, mate.

After the show I made my way to the bar to see my dad. He was standing at the same spot, wearing a slightly faraway look. It clashed with his suit. He hadn't seen me play since the early Road Runners days, though he was aware of the rock-blues music I'd been playing until I joined Mike Cotton's band. He gave me his approval with a wry smile.

'You've made it now son alright,' he said, nodding towards the stage. 'Playing with trumpets!'

He'd not only given me his approval, he'd also given me his blessing. I didn't really mind that he'd ignored the saxophone and trombone, though Nick and Boat wouldn't have been too impressed. As far as he was concerned, I was in a world-class setting and working with 'proper musicians'. It meant a lot to him. His acceptance also meant a lot to me, even though I was wearing a Rupert the Bear scarf.

Suddenly he turned towards me and quoted Benjamin Franklin: "Hide not your talent, they for we were made. What's a sundial in the shade?" He didn't really; he bought me a half of lager—which was nice.

Before we left, I was shown an article written by Viv Stanshall, the madcap singer with the equally madcap Bonzo Dog Doo Dah Band. It was regarding a recent three day stint at The Showboat, and read:

'Dear reader, I'm coming home after three days cabaret in Middlesbrough. We played in a club with surprisingly high standards. In the foyer I saw a large notice signed by the Fuhrer to the effect that: "Nobody with long hair, sideboards, or wearing dark or floral shirts would be allowed into the club". This of course excluded us as we are frightfully trendy, as you know. We were musing on this strange paradox in the life-like "bistro"-style bar when loud roaring and barking heralded the compare; a gentleman in shiny blue mohair tuxedo, very tight trousers and dark glasses ("shades", man) that lent just the right hint of intrigue and St. Tropez to his 15 stone. "Now look lads, you can't come in here looking like that, Gerroutovvit." We did, and spent three days sulking in our dressing room. By special permission only, we were allowed on stage. The club was packed every night, although this may be misleading as people tend to be fatter in the North and take up more room. But despite the rigorous entrance exam., sheep-dip and disinfectant shower provided by the management to keep out rough people and undesirables, there did seem to be a lot of punch-ups and disgorging going on amongst the elite. One night, a quite extraordinary and depressing thing happened. Three blokes came up and told us that they had shaved their sideboards and cut off their hair in order to get in to see us. I felt awful about that, but thank God it wasn't a Jewish club'.

The bouncers didn't bother me, but there again, I'd been a local lad for most of my life. It's not what you know.....

LATE-SIXTIES MUSO JOKE
A band arrived at a provincial Town Hall, and while they were unloading
their equipment the resident 'jobsworth' appeared. He quickly strove to make
an impression on the poor unsuspecting musicians.
'We've had them all here y'know. Cliff, Mike and Tina Turnip, Englebert
Humptyback, Jimi Henderson. We even had that Jazz bloke with his orches-
tra, you know… Duke o' Wellington.'
'Don't you mean Duke Ellington?' responded one of the band.
'Yes, that's him. Anyway, I don't know what they did with their money, but
none of them had two ha'pennies to rub together.'
'How'd you come to that conclusion?'
'Ah, because they were all sitting in the dressing room sharing the same
cigarette!'

Batley Variety Club was opened in March 1967 by the Batchelors and quickly established itself as Britain's premier cabaret club. It epitomised all that was expected of glamour and entertainment by presenting the biggest names in the world of showbiz—a world a million miles away from the harsh realities of Batley and its surroundings. It was an ugly area, blighted by its industrial heritage of mines and mills. God, even the soil had a layer of grime on it. At least the crap from Middlesbrough's extensive steel and chemical works could drift out over the nearby North Sea, then deposit itself into the lungs of some poor, unsuspecting crew of a Liberian-registered oil tanker (who could then dump their cargo on the unsuspecting beaches of Northern England).

We arrived in Batley on an overcast Sunday afternoon to find the place relatively deserted. I assumed that those who weren't still in the pub were watching some black and white war film staring Richard Todd on TV. The portentous atmosphere prompted the southern contingent to add, 'Serious cloth cap country. Somewhere to hide their black puddings!'

I exchanged glances with Bernie, the Manchester-born drummer, who was driving.

'And where do you lot put your jellied eels, then?' he remarked.

'Forget it Bernie, we're outnumbered,' I whispered.

We passed a group of doleful-looking locals with flowers, most likely going to the local cemetery. I almost expected to see Les Dawson being chased up the road by his mother-in-law. Thankfully, the ambience at the club was a little more uplifting.

'Oh, they love it here, y'know. All the big stars. Eartha Kitt was thinking about buying a house here.' The backstage manager said in all sincerity.

Eartha Kitt in Batley? My imagination went into overdrive.

EARTHA: 'Hi honey, gimme some of y' best soul food an' some mushy peas, my man.'

GROCER: 'Right on, chuck. Gimme five (pounds)!'

As he spoke of her intentions in the past tense, I assume she'd thought again. Maybe the tripe was below par.

I walked through to the stage area and checked out the room. It was massive. 'It'll be full every night,' assured the stage manager, who'd followed us through. Our new roadie Geoff Spooner had already set up the equipment, and after a cursory sound-check, we departed for our 'digs' in nearby Dewsbury.

Doris' guest house was on the side of a hill overlooking Dewsbury, and offered a panoramic view of the town and its surrounding areas. Why, on a clear day you could see as far as Bradford. Unfortunately there hadn't been one yet. If you liked the works of L.S. Lowry, this was definitely for you. Marge had travelled with me, so we checked into our room, which was at the back of the house, and offered exclusive views of a derelict mill and an allotment. Heating was non-existent apart from a small electric fire for fighting off the damp atmosphere. I had a feeling it would be severely put to the test. Of course, Gene didn't stay there. Heaven forbid! He was happily ensconced in his suite at the finest hotel in Leeds. Just imagine him staying at Doris' gaff ("toilet and bathroom at the end of the landing"), in his cramped attic room, shuffling down the stairs every morning for his 'fry-up'.

'Those goddamn kippers stink! And who left that leaking hot water bottle on my eiderdown?'

No, not by any stretch of it.

On the first night, I watched a bit of the support act, Bill Maynard, then a mere stand-up comedian. He was about halfway through his set when the Master Of Ceremonies ran out onto the stage and grabbed the mike.

'Pies 'ave come!' he shouted, before handing the mike back to a somewhat perplexed Maynard.

Without any further encouragement, almost every male member of the audience made a dash for the rear of the hall, where a choice of steak and kidney or meat and potato was on offer. Mr Maynard was not impressed. I prayed it didn't happen during Gene's set. They'd be looking for a new M.C. if it did.

As a novelty, somebody—Pitney or otherwise—came up with the idea of handing out questionnaires to the audience as they entered. The idea was that members of the audience could write down trivial, albeit friendly questions, such as 'How's the family?', 'I love your new record' etc, which Gene would read out during the set. He would then reciprocate on a one-to-one basis, make a fuss of the questioner, and bring an element of participation into the act. Once collected, the questionnaires would be placed on a stool at the side of the stage, to be brought on by Malcolm Cook at an arranged time. This entertaining little interlude went well until the third night, when Gene read out the first item on the pile.

'Gene, we think you are a fine looking man, but who is the hunk on bass guitar?' Laughs all round.

'Oh, that's Lem,' he replied cheerfully before picking up the next piece of paper.

'Dear Gene, which side do you dress on?' Embarrassed laughs all round. Pitney wasn't so cheerful now. I looked around at the other band members. Some of them didn't look particularly surprised. Gene looked at the next questionnaire, then put it back on the stool, before beckoning Malcolm to take it away. After the show I heard raised voices in Gene's dressing room. Soon after, the door opened and a couple of the band exited with serious faces. Malcolm shouted out after them: 'And if it ever happens again, you'll be sacked.' Naughty boys!

During the daytime, I managed to relieve the boredom by commandeering Doris' small but functional record player and playing my latest acquisition—the first Led Zeppelin album. 'They've taken over where The Yarbirds left off,' I remarked.

The other guys weren't particularly interested; they were more into Blood Sweat and Tears. I quite liked Blood Sweat and Tears, and totally disagreed with Simon Hoggart who said 'Spinning Wheel' was music to commit voluntary euthanasia by. Bernie Higgins had bought the Beatles' *White Album* during the tour and it was played a lot. I learned to play 'Blackbird' gazing out of the window at…well, blackbirds. Now I know why I never learned to play 'Albatross'.

I'd also managed to get my hands on the latest copy of *Beat Instrumental*, and was intrigued by an article on Harvey Matusaw's Jews Harp Band. Describing a typical recording session for their album, *The Wars Between The Fats and the Thins*, it went on: "The only guitar in sight is an acoustic with no back and only two strings that Anna is waving round in front of a mike. Blonde-haired Lesley is sitting on a stool scraping a hooter across a zither. She abandons the hooter in favour of a bell. She also sings and plays anything including clockwork aeroplane. Chris, Rod and 78-year-old Claude are filling the studio with a strange humming sound that goes "woing woing woing". I secretly wished I had a copy. There's only so many times you can listen to 'Spinning Wheel'.

Peter the pianist seemed like a man with a fine prospect of happiness behind him. He just couldn't win, either at the roulette wheel or, as it turned out, in his pursuit of the opposite sex. Unbeknownst to the rest of us, he'd had his eye on Doris all week. Unfortunately for him, so had somebody else. On our last night she came to see the show, and afterwards travelled back with us to the digs. As she'd given up her room to accommodate us all, she had to sleep downstairs in the lounge. So, bearing this in mind, we'd usually have a quick cup of tea or a snack, then go to our respective rooms. This night was no different, except we were able to say goodnight to her. She returned the sentiment and retired to the lounge for a well earned sleep. Or so we were led to believe. In reality, she'd been chatted up by one of the band, who sneaked back down soon after. Within no time, they were writhing around the room with unbridled passion. Soon they were jammed up against the door, and going at it hammer and tong. Suddenly there was a gentle knock on the door behind them, and Peter the pianist requesting: 'Doris, can I come in?' Severe coitis interuptus followed. Once again: 'Doris, can I come in?' and an attempted entry while the band member's member suffered an unexpected exit. Luckily, the combined weight of the lovers prevented any further embarrassment as Peter the pianist accepted defeat and trudged back upstairs. The atmosphere during our final breakfast was somewhat strained, and I'm certain the poor bastard never learned the identity of his amorous usurper.

I was still at Doris' when I discovered that an Island Records 'sampler' LP called *You Can All Join In* had entered the Top Ten in the album charts. Included was 'Pearly Queen' by Tramline. Fame at last! Pity the band no longer existed. We could have strutted around Middlesbrough going 'We're in the Top Ten, nyaah, nyaah!' Actually, I think we'd have acted really cool.

John McCoy might have said: 'Yeah man, it's a real gas to be in the chart. We're gonna get our heads together at a little cottage near Robin Hood's Bay, then maybe check out California.'

I could see the headline in the *Evening Gazette*:

"LOCAL LADS OFF TO SEEK FAME AND FORTUNE IN THE CUT-THROAT WORLD OF POP. EX-GAZETTE EMPLOYEE TO TRY FOR A SECOND TIME".

A few years later, John McCoy helped another local lad to fame and fortune (in the cut-throat etc). His name was Chris Rea—and still is.

When In Rome.... or Was It Sweden?

One thing I'd discovered about being a professional musician was the total lack of continuity. How about this: Finish at Batley Variety Club on the Saturday night, travel to Bexley in Kent on the Sunday for a gig at the Black Prince, then have two days off in London. Travel to Belgium on the Wednesday for a gig at Shape Military Base in Mons, then on to Rome via Bologna for a fortnight's residency at the Titan Club. This kind of itinerary wouldn't suit everyone, especially introverted accountants or unambitious traffic wardens. Of course, when you're only eighteen, with an artistic bent and a sense of adventure, it's the most enviable of occupations.

However, if you're forty eight, a bent artist, and suffering from bouts of agoraphobia, your feelings may be a little more ambivalent. Nevertheless, crossing the Alps was a memorable experience, and the drive through the Brenner Pass was breathtaking. I took my turn in the van for part of the journey with another member of the band and Geoff the roadie, who remained at the wheel throughout. To assist him in yielding to the lures of the Sandman, he'd popped a couple of 'uppers'. When I asked him how he was feeling, he smiled broadly and answered with wide-eyed sincerity: 'I feel great! I love everyone!' Right on, Hannibal.

Thieves respect property. They merely wish the property to become their property that they more perfectly respect it—G.K. Chesterton.

We arrived in Rome on the afternoon of the first gig, and called at the Titan Club for accommodation details. I may have been disorientated from the mammoth journey or just dumb, but I made a costly mistake. Thinking there was somebody still in the car, I left the door open and headed towards a nearby café for a coke. Wrong. A few minutes later somebody shouted: 'Who left the car door open?' My brain did a quick car scan. That lovely old World War Two full length leather coat that I'd bought at Kensington Market prior to the Pitney tour was in the back seat. Not any more, mate. I spent the rest of the day cursing "those thieving fucking bastards". There was one consolation—the weather was nice, so I wouldn't be needing an overcoat. And if I was to respect that old adage, "When in Rome do as the Romans do", I'd best make a start with the coat pockets in the cloakroom that night. I didn't, of course—my moral fibre wouldn't allow it.

On one of the days off, prior to our epic Alpen crossing, I'd treated myself to a Cry-Baby 'Wah Wah' pedal a la Eric Clapton and Jimi Hendrix, and had incorporated it into a couple of songs. After one of the sets, a middle-aged guy, who could easily have been a member of the Cosa Nostra or a lawyer approached me.

'Hey, dat'a pedala you usin' reminda me ofa de trumpet players when deya use a de mute.' I think he may have been Italian.

I toyed with the idea of asking him if he was in the 'mob', and that if any of his friends or associates came across some twat wearing a dark green World War Two full-length leather coat they had my permission to cement him into the next motorway bridge. I bottled out in the end, but listen: If the little shit who nicked my coat in Rome in April 1969 is reading this, just keep looking over your shoulder, pal—your days are numbered.

Rome is a beautiful city. One afternoon we did the tourist bit and visited the Coliseum, that place where they raced their chariots, and some other impressive tourist spots. Sorry, I can't be more explicit, but I'm only good at remembering thefts. On another sunny afternoon, we made for St. Peter's Square, and looked around the Sistine Chapel, famed for its painted ceiling courtesy of Michelangelo. There were lots of small groups being guided by be-spectacled women or bearded men. Or was it be-spectacled men or bearded... I listened in on one of them.

"Michelangelo was no angel himself. He was convinced that Pope Julius the second would find some crafty way of seeing the paintings before they were finished. The story goes that the Pope, disguised as a workman, slipped into the Chapel under cover of darkness and ascended the scaffolding to have a peek. Unfortunately, he stumbled across the great artist, who had taken to sleeping up there to foil precisely this sort of spying mission. Furious, he hurled planks at the intruder, who departed cursing. When Michelangelo learned it was the Pope, he fled the city in fear."

An English tourist, gazing up at one of the genius' greatest works, The Creation of Adam, remarked: 'Hey, that Adam wasn't very well hung, was he?'

His wife whacked him on the arm and said, 'He was an icon, not a blue movie star!'

I slept in on Easter Sunday and missed the Pope's address. Of course, I never mentioned this to my mother—she'd have been mortified.

Back home, I read an interview in the *Melody Maker* with B.B. King, the great American blues performer, after a concert at the Royal Albert Hall. His humility and underdeveloped ego made a refreshing change, as he shared his enthusiasm for the British blues players, namely Eric Clapton and Peter Green. He admitted that his nervousness at playing such a prestigious venue caused him to break two strings. "I very seldom break a guitar string, only when I'm nervous. And I only changed them last week". I hoped he didn't adopt the same attitude towards his underwear. Seriously though, his *Live At The Regal* album was a milestone in blues performances, and a must for any guitarist. And who was his favourite guitar player? Surprise, surprise—Monsieur Reinhardt, of course! Everybody loves Django.

Good news came via Geoff the roadie, who invited me and Marge to share a cottage with him—meaning freedom from Finsbury Park. The only downside was that the new 'pad' was in Hoddesdon in Hertfordshire, a good twenty miles from London, and I didn't drive. However, as long as we both held our positions with the band, I'd be guaranteed a lift to the gigs; and if I needed to get to London for any other business, well, the Green Line bus company offered a good service. Anyhow, back on the one-nighter circuit, the band played the rather oddly named Normal College in Bangor. I honestly can't remember if it was normal or otherwise, but nothing stands out in my mind. It's not difficult to conjure up images of smart but casually dressed students going about their business in an orderly fashion, behaving themselves, and maybe letting their hair down a bit on the dance night.

A couple of months after our return from Rome, we were off overseas again, this time to meet our liberal-minded (nudge-nudge, wink-wink) brothers and sisters in Sweden. We were to spend almost a month backing former Manfred Mann singer Paul Jones. Flying to Stockholm via Copenhagen, it was my first time on a plane. I was nervous, and still am. If we were meant to fly, God would have given us Valium.

All the shows took place in Folk Parks, popular summer locations and ideal for outdoor gigs. As usual, Lucas had the easiest job; get changed, sing two or three songs, get unchanged, then search for the nearest half-cut salesman to blag drinks from. And judging by the price of the drinks, he was going to have his work cut out. Mugging them might have been a better option.

Paul travelled separately with his tour manager, an ex-boxer called Billy, who had the nose to prove it. Our driver and tour manager was an ageing Swede called Jay Elwing, who looked like a cross between Aristotle Onassis and Mister Pastry. He drove us around in an American, four-wheel-drive van with a trailer for the equipment that put the early Road Runners to shame, though we were in a slightly different league.

Poor Jay was a bit too highly-strung for this lark and would often become agitated, spitting out odd curses like: 'Shit on my arsehole!' and 'Fuck at the car!' He told us he was an ex-jazz musician who'd turned to tour managing to supplement his income, found steady work and never returned to his chosen occupation. I found it odd, but throughout the whole tour he never once yearned to pick up one of the brass instruments and have a blow. I assumed he was a saxophone player, but maybe he played vibes, or piano. Or there again, perhaps he was a shit player who'd found his true vocation—driving mad Englishmen round his country.

It could have been worse, or even Latvia. Sweden in the Summertime is a glorious place to be once you're out of the city. Miles of natural forest, thousands of lakes, breathtaking sunsets, wild elk, and hot dogs called 'korvs'. Lem Lubin developed such a craving for the latter that he was re-named Lemmie Korv. Jay Elwing thought he was "Shitting fuck crazy!" I thought he'd be shitting fuck fat if he wasn't careful.

We soon discovered that the impressive American wagon had one drawback. There were two small windows on the roof which could be opened to allow extra air to circulate. They were put to good use until somebody disposed of their cigarette through the forward one, an action that was to cause unexpected activity in Nick Newell's groin area. The discarded ciggie had set sail from one window, entered the other, and come to rest in the sax players crotch. A minute later, we were alerted to the poor man's dilemma by his sudden cry of extreme surprise and the spectacle of a small plume of smoke rising from his flies.

'Who the bloody hell did that?' he cried.

'Must have come from the car in front,' a guilty voice suggested.

'The nearest car's over half a mile away,' countered the aggrieved Nick.

'Strong breezes over them lakes,' was the pathetic response.

I was aware of the 'Sexy Sweden' tag before we arrived. A country with legalised pornography and a large ratio of stunning-looking women could hardly be ignored, and therefore weren't. The porn was hardly tactful placed, as it would eventually be in designated sex shops in Germany. In Sweden it was displayed in newsagents' windows on the lower shelves beneath Auto Trader and Fishing World. A bit of a shock for us British, but nothing to the indigenous who seemed blasé. I thought about the priest who'd endorsed my visa photograph. What would he have made of it all?

Though I wasn't particularly interested in 'pulling', a week or so into the tour I found myself in the company of a young beauty, and the mutual attraction was becoming too much to bear. We were just about to head for the hotel when she admitted that she was only fourteen. Now, I was still only eighteen myself, but I was old enough to go to jail for the next five years, and I didn't fancy spending them with a bunch of psychotic Vikings. I'd leave that kind of gamble to Jerry Lee Lewis when he passed through town.

"Goodnight little Anifrid. Get yourself straight home, now!"

Paul Jones had chosen an interesting selection of songs to perform. We did the obvious Manfred Mann hits like 'Pretty Flamingo' and 'If You Gotta Go, Go Now', his own hits 'High Time' and 'I've Been A Bad Bad Boy', and a rather dramatic rendition of Country Joe and the Fish's anti-Vietnam War song, 'Fixin' To Die Rag'. At its climax, Paul would drop to the floor apparently having been shot. This little bit of theatre stayed in the set until one particular night when, resplendent in a pair of brand new, expensively cut grey velvet trousers, he 'died' atop a rather large patch of wet paint which some careless stagehand had hurriedly overlooked. It left a huge stain down one leg. Given that the offending pigment was deep red, the effect was stunningly realistic. Paul was neither convinced, impressed nor amused, and from then on, the song was performed without the death scene. It just wasn't the same after that.

I persuaded Paul to perform a B-side from another one of his singles, an off-the-wall track called 'The Dog Presides', which had Jeff Beck on guitar. As the original had no brass section, the lads could have a breather whilst I attempted my Beck licks—a bit of expression in a set now devoid of death scenes. I'd hoped that Paul would invent another dramatic exit, one which didn't require him to hit the deck, such as being turned into a pillar of salt, or getting vaporized in an atomic bomb explosion, but alas, it never materialised.

Being a good lad I wrote to my family back in Middlesbrough on a number of occasions to keep them informed of my Scandanavian adventures (well, most of them). From the Hotel Knaust in Sundsvall: 'I'm writing this letter at 12.15.am. It never seems to get dark here, especially in the north. The darkest it gets is like dawn in England. By 1.am it will be quite light, and at 3.am it will be light. The tour is going well. Paul is very popular over here. We get on well with him. The kids don't scream, they just applaud loudly at the end of every number. The one which seems to go down the best is a blues number, and some of the people actually clap the guitar solos! We are staying in the best hotels, they are really suave. The one in Gothenburg even had music in the lifts.'

As a P.S. I wrote: 'The stamps here are strawberry flavoured.' I bet the condoms were too.

During the tour we went way up in the northern reaches, far away from the big cities (all three of them), and stopped for a spot of lunch. We were just finishing our roll mop herring baguette or whatever, when a lovely, old silver-haired couple approached our table. The old man said something quietly in Swedish, then took Lucas' hand and gently squeezed it, before returning to his wife. They furnished us with another sweet smile, then walked out of the restaurant hand in hand. We were confused, not least Lucas, who opened his hand to reveal a small silver coin.

'What was all that about, man?' he asked Jay.

'It's a local custom,' explained the tour manager. 'You are the first black man they have ever seen in the flesh, and by giving you something silver, they are guaranteed good luck.'

'And what have I been guaranteed?' enquired Lucas.

'The equivalent of about twenty cents,' came the reply.

I think Lucas said, 'Damn!' (pronounced 'Daiyamm!'). Yes, there's definitely nowt so queer as folk.

Before we left Sweden we recorded a few songs for a TV programme, then returned to Blighty, where we made our way to the BBC studios in Maida Vale to make ourselves known on the airwaves. Alexis Korner was a bit odd. The father of the British blues boom was a raspy-voiced Greek-

Russian who always seemed to be smoking something. He eventually died of lung cancer. When I finally got to meet him, he was presenting a rhythm and blues show for the World Service. Knowing Lucas and the Mike Cotton Sound, we probably had a gig in Durham or somewhere the same night. Anyway, we recorded two or three songs and were just about to leave when Alexis called me over to a small recording booth off the main studio.

'Hey man, what keys were the songs in?' Strange request, I thought. Still, who was I to question such a legendary figure.

I gave him the required information, then stood back to observe his next step, which was to record his intros by strumming his acoustic guitar in the key of the impending song. As he faded the song in, he faded his guitar out. I suppose you could say it was a novel idea. Or an idea for a novel, though it would have been rather short and uninteresting.

"Alexis faded the track in, and his guitar out. Fifteen minutes later he went home. The End".

In July 1969, Mick Taylor made his debut with the Rolling Stones, and I was still playing 'Ride Your Pony'. Life just wasn't fair! Life was also still Sixties-mad. Consider these snippets of information from the *Melody Maker*'s 'Raver' column that same month:

"Why were the Bonzo Dog Band chasing their handsome, debonair manager Tony Stratton-Smith, across a deserted Cork Football Stadium last week?

And:

"Viv Stanshall amazed Belfast by parading the streets in bathing draws and shouting "wardrobe" and "porcupine fat—quickly!""

Or:

Jiving K. Boots plans all nude tour of the US Southern States lecturing on Lenin, Marx, Humanism, Tolerance and the health dangers of short haircuts. "I expect it to go down a bomb," he said last night from a mental home in Penge." There'd be a few more in there with him before the decade was out.

Note: Jiving K.Boots was the creation of journalist Chris Welch—or was it the other way round?

On the twentieth, we were driving back from the Carlton Club, Warrington—yes, the place where Tramline were paid off a year earlier— when a newsflash on the radio informed us that man had landed on the Moon. Fantastic! If they needed volunteers to colonise the place there were plenty of bloody lunatics running around England and Ireland for a start; and, apparently, at some place called Woodstock.

An Itch In Time . . . .

Having been formally educated to the fact that, "We beat them three times—two wars and a World Cup final," I looked forward to my first visit to Germany (then only the Western half) with time-honoured feelings of excitement and trepidation. Two weeks at the PN Club in Munich, performing three sets a night and staying on the other side of Leopold Strasse at the two-bed roomed apartment provided by the club's owner, Peter Neumann. Now, eight into two doesn't really go, even if the two are quite spacious. A power trio without a roadie would have been extremely happy with this arrangement, and one-hit-wonder busker Don Partridge would have been able to accommodate his whole family and Earth Wind and Fire's road crew. We just mucked in, and as I've mentioned before, when you're only eighteen nothing really bothers you apart from spots. Or crabs.

Sitting in the back of the band's Ford Granada somewhere in Belgium, I felt a natural urge to scratch one of my hairy legs. Well, if I'd have scratched somebody else's I would have looked a right prat, wouldn't I? And apart from that, nobody else knew where the itch was. Soon the irritation became more intense and, ominously, more widespread. Sitting in a crowded car with one trouser leg rolled up like some sort of disorientated freemason dispelled any thoughts I'd had on concealing my quandary. It didn't take long for the others to become aware of my obvious discomfort, and about a nano-second more to establish the cause.

'You've got crabs!' exclaimed a horrified voice as Bernie Higgins almost lost control of the car.

'Is that bad then?' I enquired in a pathetic, semi-apologetic way.

Silly question; they may as well have handed me a bell and a sign proclaiming 'UNCLEAN' if their expressions were anything to go by.

'Just bloody roll your trousers down and tuck them into your socks. And stay that way 'till we get to Munich.'

Now, the subject of body lice usually crops up in conversations about social diseases, but I can honestly say that I'd had absolutely no contact with unfamiliar women in the time leading up to our departure. However, a few days earlier we'd played at Redruth in Cornwall where we'd spent the night at a less than salubrious hotel. In fact, it was a lorry driver's hostel at the back of a petrol station. Limited as I was in the field of overnight accommodation, it soon became apparent that the fare on offer was not going to win any awards for comfort, cleanliness and modern appliances, though it did have a 'shilling a go' gas fire. And the bed seemed to have been made but not changed….Hmmm. The next morning I passed on the breakfast—which looked like it had been cooked in boiling tar and regurgitated by a deranged skunk—and headed home as normal as Norman (my recently acquired band nickname). As I scratched my way through the remainder of Belgium and into Germany, I mulled over the new-found knowledge that a local chemist would supply me with the mother of all ointments. 'It'll burn your bollocks off!' the others informed me with more than a touch of sadistic glee. What a start. Still, sod it, it couldn't get any worse. Oh, yes it could—oh, yes it did!

We arrived in Munich mid-evening, and due to my position as host to the ugly bug ball-clingers, I was awarded pariah status in the shared bedroom, a position that required me to move my bed as far away from the other three sharers as possible. Once settled into outcast's corner, I resisted the urge to pacify my multitude of itches, and joined the rest of the guys in search of food. This was the band's second residency at the PN, so they were on familiar turf and knew the local eating places, in particular The Wiennerwald. This popular chain of restaurants offered quality food at reasonable prices, with a lively atmosphere created to a certain extent by the waitresses—busty frauleins carrying armfuls of beer. Of course, the menu was in German so I didn't have a clue what to ask for.

'Try the Huhnerbruste,' suggested Boat. 'It's chicken breast in a curry sauce with rice.'

'Sounds good to me,' I replied, scratching my groin. The others moved as one in the opposite direction to where I was sitting. Bernie at least offered some sympathy. 'Tomorrow I'll take you to the chemists, they call it the apotheke here, and we'll get you sorted out.'

I nodded my thanks in an itchy sort of way, then glancing around noticed that many of the local men were wearing breeches tucked into long socks. Surely they hadn't all contracted crabs as well? I was assured it was part of the traditional Bavarian dress which also included short leather pants and small brimmed hats with feathers. Ooooh, nice! We ate heartily, then retired for a well-earned, travel weary sleep, and though my parasitic friends tried their hardest to keep me awake (I'm talking about the body lice, not the guys in the band), I soon drifted off.

I woke up in the middle of the night and knew immediately that something was wrong. An overwhelming sense of nausea had gripped my insides, like a maelstrom of army boots trying to kick their way out of my gut. Surprise soon gave way to reality and within seconds I'd deduced that

a) I hadn't been attacked,

b) something was trying to get out of my body, and

c) the film The Alien had yet to be conceived.

A huge neon sign suddenly blinded in my mind's eye .... FOOD POISONING! Until that mind-engraving moment, my only experience of gastric disorders had been endured with vapid resentment during a family holiday at a timeworn bed and breakfast hotel in Blackpool. On that occasion there was every likelihood that my condition was elevated by criminally inadequate kitchen hygiene and/or a suspicious looking lamb chop, though taking into account my mother's frequent comments regarding the amount of dog hairs around the place, there was always the nagging possibility that I'd nurtured a fur ball. Ten years later, another animal had been in cahoots with human negligence to create even more havoc in my abdominal tract. Never trust a Bavarian with a chicken.

I somehow managed to negotiate a successful path to the bathroom without waking, or indeed soiling, my slumbering room-mates, and managed to assume the release position a nano-second before the onslaught began. Without wishing to exaggerate the magnitude of my anal emission, all I'll say is that I finally understood that joke about the Brown Windsor soup. God, there must have been a tureen of it. Then, just when I thought it was all over, my intestines decided to put on a bit of a show:

LARGE COLON: Right Laddie, I think a change in consistency is called for here. Preseeeent, medium-hard stool!
SMALL COLON: Yes, Sir!

ME: Oooh, ahhh, groan, etc.
LARGE COLON: Same again, bombadier!
SMALL COLON: Coming up, Sir!
ME: Gor, I feel sick.

Instinctively, I stood up, turned round, and dropped to the toilet bowl where I came face to faeces with the former Bavarian chicken speciality, just in time to add my own speciality vomit topping—the Devil's trifle. For anybody who's never poked their nose into their own discarded stomach contents, I can tell you that it's a once in a lifetime experience. And whoever designed those high-shelved Teutonic toilets was a debased pervert. After the deluge I sat back, spent and dispirited, on that unfamiliar bathroom floor, engulfed in a wave of melancholy; that sad, desolate emotion I'd experienced in hospital, at the summer camp, and in Finsbury Park with The Wildflowers. From home-sick to poxy badly-cooked chicken twat of a chef-sick. Eventually, I managed to drag myself back to bed, with only my body lice for company. Somewhere in Chicago, the down-hearted blues singer was still better off than me.

I awoke un-refreshed and full of joie de mort. My head ached, my stomach felt like It'd been punched repeatedly by Henry Cooper, my arse stung, I had a taste in my mouth like I'd been French-kissing a camel; and the parasites were digging in like Tommies at Ypres. The rest of the guys, unaware of my toilet trauma, urged me to visit the chemists pronto or face banishment to Crab Island. Bernie, true to his word, led me across the road to the apotheke, creating in me a sense of reassurance.

'I know a couple of words in German—leave it to me.'

Good bloke. He headed straight for the counter whilst I surveyed the hairbrush rack. 'Mittel fur lousen, bitte,' he asked the stern looking lady assistant. She gave him a slightly horrified look which prompted Bernie to turn around and point his finger directly at me. 'For him!' he proclaimed.

The bastard! A woman near to me gave out what I can only describe as a suppressed scream, then hurried out of the shop. The Brünhilde behind the counter, still taken aback by the original request, now directed her attention to the spineless outcast by the brush collection.

'Ze lotion is to be applied twice,' she eyed me contemptuously, 'no, four times a day, until ze scourge is eliminated.'

I settled for three, and let me tell you it was painful. The pests weren't really killed off; more like incinerated. Yes, Joe Bradley, I know—it was all part of my education.

British Joke Regarding The Lack Of German Humour
WILHELM: Knock, knock.
FRITZ: Who's there?
WILHELM: Gunter.
FRITZ: Hello, Gunter.

The clientele at the PN Club was the usual mix of regulars and in-town-for-the-night merchants, and as the first of the three sets was usually a bit on the sparse side, it could be used to try out new songs. The band's repertoire of cover versions guaranteed that the portable record player back at the apartment could be put to good use. Lucas would come in with a new soul album, the other guys would put on the latest Chicago Transit Authority or Buddy Miles Express, and I turned up with Jeff Beck's new release, *Beck Ola*, or Joe Cocker. Lucas or the others would win hands down, but it didn't worry me—time was one my side! Don't forget, it was all part of my …etc.

This was great experience and fun, especially as I was now totally in control of my motions, and my pubic areas were, once more, free from unwanted visitors. I celebrated with a chocolate milk. The club's DJ's choice of music reminded us that the punters were not just here to do the wild uninhibited Frug; they liked to listen too. Lucas enjoyed 'I Heard It Through The Grapevine' as much as I enjoyed Fleetwood Mac's 'Man Of The World', and the odd track from *Blues From Laurel Canyon* by John Mayall and the Bluesbreakers. There seemed to be quite a few requests for 'Je T'aime' by Jane Birkin and that French bloke—most of them, I suspect, from certain members of the band whose ribald comments during Jane's breathy divulgements placed them firmly into the collective known as 'the lads'. The DJ even played 'Sugar Sugar' by the Archies once, but was at pains to let everyone know that it was not his personal choice. As he'd just played 'Honky Tonk Women' and a track by Johnny Winter, I was inclined to believe him.

Munich was fast gaining a reputation as the cultural city in Germany, attracting a wide variety of artists, actors , musicians, hippies and weirdos. They presented a very interesting contraposition to the middle class and often very right wing Bavarians. This clash of attitudes was evident on my first stroll round the old town centre in search of a recommended currywurst. After a few minutes, I came across an American hippy being hassled by a middle-aged shopkeeper with a dopamine deficiency.

'Get from mien door, you unwashed!' bellowed the sour kraut.

'Hey, cool man it man,' remonstrated the hairy one, 'life's too short.'

Moving away, the dude sought reassurance in my presence.

'Hi,' he smiled.

'Hello, do you know where I can get a currywurst?' I asked.

'Hey, man, I'm herbivorous,' he replied, somewhat taken-aback by my request.

'Oh, hello Herb, do you know where I can get a currywurst?'

He turned and fled; two arseholes in one day was enough as far as he was concerned. I remained baffled by his abrupt exit until one of the band enlightened my font of knowledge to the ways of the vegetarian. Yes, Joe, I know.

Oldham on a Saturday afternoon was a bit of an anti-climax after a fortnight in groovy Munich. In fact, Oldham was always going to be an anti-climax, no matter where we'd been. However, the band had devised a method of light relief that guaranteed some great moments of piss-taking—the game of Cloth Caps and Trilbys. The object of the game was to count the numbers of cloth caps vs trilbys worn by the masculine population of the main shopping area of Oldham on a Saturday afternoon. I experienced this recreational gem twice, and can boast that 'Cloth Cap Corner' was my highest-scoring sighting. Here, at this local shrine to the war dead, old men would gather to have a good moan beneath the names of some of those who gave their lives for juvenile delinquents, Third-World spongers drawing supplementary benefit for four wives and their children back home, and piss-taking musicians. I was awarded nine points for that one. Needless to say, being in deepest Lancashire, the cloth caps always won. And the trilbied types always looked hen-pecked. I think it might have been a different story in Henley-on-Thames.

Mike Cotton was a bit of a musical pioneer. He'd formed his own trad-jazz band, the Mike Cotton Jazzmen, at the onset of the Sixties when traditionalists like Acker Bilk and Kenny Ball realised that there was money to be made from pairing pretty pop tunes with New Orleans-style jazz arrangements. Two or three years later he managed to ride the tide of R&B by sliding into the currant vogue via the Mike Cotton

Sound, featuring Dave Rowberry, who later joined the Animals. By 1966 the trend had given way to sweet soul music, spearheaded in Britain by Geno Washington and the Ram Jam Band. Enter one authentic front man—Lucas. Throughout the numerous changes in personnel, only one original member, John Beecham, had weathered the storm with Mike. Who said trombones went out with George Chisholm? Now it was time for another musical metamorphosis; and for me, a personal one as well— Marge confirmed that she was pregnant. We were a little surprised to say the least, but at that age—and particularly in that age—life was full of surprises!

Anybody who claims to have been party to the club scene of the mid-Sixties but can't recall Zoot Money, wasn't there at all. The expression 'character' could almost have been defined for George Bruno 'Zoot' Money. Though he would have been the first to admit to being influenced by Ray Charles, his own madcap personality broke new grounds. A true 'raver', he didn't give a damn about convention, and, I'm pleased to say, still doesn't. His Big Roll Band were a talented bunch, and featured a young blond guitarist who was playing an original Gibson Les Paul Standard before Eric Clapton—Andy Summers, way before he helped form Police. I might be wrong but I have a feeling that Clapton bought the Les Paul from him and used it on the now historical Bluesbreakers album—yes, that one.

As we all know, Zoot ditched the Big Roll Band in '67 when he succumbed to psychedelia and formed Dantalion's Chariot with Andy Summers and Big Roll Band's drummer Colin Allen. They performed in white robes, used white instruments and amplifiers, and released a single entitled 'Madman Running through the Fields'. Audiences soon came to the conclusion that real ale was not their prime creative influence. Shortly afterwards, Zoot moved to California to join his parter in crime Eric Burdon in the New Animals. Here endeth the history lesson.

Zoot returned to Britain in the Autumn of 1969, a mellower man raring to go. He spoke to Nick Newall who in turn spoke to Mike. The next thing, our leader informed us that the band needed to progress (as in progresive rock), and it was going to be Zoot Money and The Mike Cotton Sound. We all agreed that it was, with great respect to Lucas, a move in the right direction. It transpired that Lucas was very philosophical about the whole thing and no bad blood was spilt. The guy was a trooper; he just got on with it. Nick was back with his old boss, who was full of ideas, the brass section could stretch out into the realms of Blood, Sweat and Tears, Bernie and Lem could chill-out on some new rhythms, and I could do a bit more solo work. Unfortunately, it didn't work out.

Maybe people expected too much from Zoot. The old looner was still in there somewhere, but the man had moved on. Now there was a deeper aspect to his character, especially when he performed pieces like Judy Collins''Both Sides Now' and 'Leonard Cohen's 'Story of Isaac'. However, just as people were readying themselves to adopt the cross-legged 'sitting and listening position', he'd launch into an exhilarating version of the Beatles''Blackbird', complete with simultaneous manic soloing from the brass players. Then, once the unprompted witticisms started, it was into 'Big Time Operator' and vintage Zoot a la the Flamingo Club.

I loved Zoot and got on well with him; he had a musical outlook and a strength of character that had to be admired. So, early in 1970, when Mike announced plans to transform the Mike Cotton Sound into Satisfaction, I decided to stay with Zoot in his new, pared-down line-up. To be honest, I don't remember too much from that Zoot/Mike Cotton period, though one gig stands out in my mind. We played an all-nighter at the Lyceum in London with Ten Years After and East Of Eden, and during Ten Years After's set I was washing my hands in the public toilet when a young black guy asked me who was on stage.

'It's Ten Years After,' I answered helpfully.

'Sounds more like ten years too fucking late to me!' he replied.

Ah, well, you can't please everybody.

Madman Wading Through A Sea Of Mars Bars

To coincide with Zoot's new phase, his publicist issued a new press release. Under the heading 'All hope abandon, ye who enter the head of Money', he was described thus: "That thick thatch of flaming ginger frizz that sprang from that head. And the cherubic-demonic face grew in front of it, too. But the stuff inside the head of Money remains a black, festering secret. The man himself is one of those complexities you find cackling away under the tables at four in the morning; the one in the black cape and evil laugh when you're stoned".

Though I'd only known Zoot a short time, it's fair to say that the writer had presented a relatively accurate profile, apart from his pre-occupation with the colour black. To my knowledge, none of his festering secrets were black—and neither was his cape. It was a striking shade of burgundy, in crushed velvet.

Whoever thinks of going to bed before twelve o'clock is a scoundrel
—Samuel Johnson.

Zoot lived on the ground floor of a large Victorian terraced house in Gunter Grove, close to West Kensington tube station with his wife Ronni, a relative of Lulu. They'd adopted a bit of an open-house policy were people were always welcome, though I think I'd missed out on the under-the-table nights by a few years. Times were, by now, a little more, er, transitional. The new band was a four-piece, featuring Zoot, Barry Dean on bass, Barry Wilson on drums, and myself on Telecaster, still lugging that bloody Impact gear around, though I think I'd temporarily dispensed with one of the 4x12 speaker cabinets. Zoot was playing what he described as "The only travelling Fender Rhodes electric piano in the country". It was a beautiful looking instrument with a gorgeous, warm tone. The lower half housed two large speakers which could 'pan' the tremolo into a stereo effect. The equipment travelled in a short-wheel-base Ford Transit van commandeered by Johnny Mac, a relative of Zoot and Ronni, a very sound bloke who'd perfected a great repartee with Zoot, and a bloody good roadie to boot. It seemed that Zoot was the only driver in the band, so he was lumbered with the task of getting us to and from the gigs, which he did—on a Californian driving licence. If the police had stopped him he'd have had to adopt a West Coast twang. Luckily they didn't, and we were spared the Venice Beach boy/Malibu Beach bum impersonations.

Zoot had been at the forefront of the mid-Sixties night club, and that often meant all-night, club scene, where prescription pills and the odd Scotch and Coke had been the staple diet of the raver. Possible indulgence may have been the influence behind these two classic Moneyisms:

1) After one particular heavy night he described his condition as 'Like wading through a sea of Mars Bars.'

2) 'I can't decide whether I want to go up, go down, or sort of wobble about in the middle!'

After a few days rehearsal above a pub in Chiswick High Road, the cool little combo set off on its travels. The musical direction was pioneered by Zoot alone (as opposed to Zoot Alors!), though the three musketeers were encouraged to put forward any ideas that might avail the "black festering secret" that lurked in the corridors of Zoot's head. He decided to keep 'Blackbird', 'Both Sides Now', and 'Story Of Isaac' from the previous set-up, and added the Band's 'Up On Cripple Creek', plus some Zoot originals and newly-written material by up and coming writers. One of these songs, 'The Days I Will Remember', by Tony Colton and Ray Smith from the band Head, Hands and Feet, was a wistful ballad in the key of A minor. It occurred to me that the main theme from the second movement (the slow one) from the Concierto De Aranjuez by Rodrigo, more commonly known as the Guitar Concerto, could possibly be used as an intro to the song. I played it on my classical guitar and the idea was accepted, serving as my contribution to progressive rock and a definite improvement on 'Mazurka!' Nowadays it might be regarded as pretentious. In general, the set was a musical hybrid of melodic, down-home, and out-there songs performed by an eccentric, ever-so-slightly manic bandleader, and three keen, respectful, trouble-free young chaps. Ah, the nostalgia of it all.

I reserve very little of that nostalgia for one of the band's first gigs, at a small basement club in Whitley Bay, a seaside resort near Newcastle. For a start, there was no stage. This presented us with the disadvantage of having to stand eyeball to eyeball with the people directly in front of us, who were mainly disinterested young men out on the piss. Hovering directly above their heads was a thick pall of cigarette smoke which gradually descended upon them like a Victorian fog, giving them the appearance of an inquisitive crowd at a Jack the Ripper murder scene. Everybody in the place seemed to be smoking at least two cigarettes each, including the industrious bar staff.

Years later I came across a quote from one Samuel de Sorbiere; it read: "The English are naturally lazy, and spend half of their time in taking Tobacco". He obviously didn't visit Whitley Bay, where they seemed to spend all of their time in taking it. They should have had caged beagles playing there. One ignorant sod, standing directly in front of Zoot, turned around, sat on the piano, and started chatting to his mates, completely unaware that he was doing so on "The only travelling Fender Rhodes electric piano in the country". And Whitley Bay. Zoot reacted immediately and pushed the cretin away. He disappeared into the nicotine haze like a dejected Heathcliffe. After the gig I didn't even bother to have a fag; after two hours in that place I could already feel the first twinges of emphysema. A girl with callus's on her knees started chatting to me, then pulled me into a nearby cupboard. What a bloody mad place! I left with a satisfied smile and an irritating cough.

A few weeks later we embarked on short tour with John Mayall's Bluesbreakers, whose line-up was unusual to say the least. Mayall on organ, guitar, harmonica and vocals; Alex Dmochowski on bass; Jon Mark on nylon string guitar; and Johnny Almond on saxes. No drums! Most unusual. Also on the bill was Duster Bennett, a brilliant one-man blues band who was signed to the Blue Horizon label, and a good friend of Peter Green. The venues were highly respectable places like Manchester Free Trade Hall, the Usher Hall Edinburgh and the City Hall in Newcastle. From the onset it was plain to see that apart from Mayall, the rest of his band were a little frayed round the edges, or, to put it more politely, tired and emotional. At the outset of their performance at the Sheffield City Hall, the stage was bereft of one bass player until Mr Dmochowski came dashing on, plugged in and started to adjust his amplifier settings. This prompted the somewhat unimpressed Mayall to announce: 'That's Alex Dmchowski, who has adopted the professional habit of always being late on stage.' Oooh. A couple of nights later in the communal dressing room, Mark blasted Almond for playing an upright piano. Unaware of the condition known as stress, I looked on, somewhat perplexed.

After Edinburgh, Zoot drove us to Aberdeen for the next show. Somewhere in the wilds of the highlands, we stopped for a refreshment break at a small but welcoming café. The building also housed a gift shop selling local delicacies, like those oatcakes that are made from sawdust, and genuine Scottish fudge made in Islamabad. Pooh-poohing such tawdry bric-a-brac with a contemptible sniff, I eventually emerged from the building sporting a bright red tartan tam-o'-shanter and carrying a shepherd's crook. Feeling suitably attired, I suggested that a wee walk in the nearest glen could be beneficial to us all. Surprisingly, my partners in silliness agreed, and for a short while we roved the hillsides as self-proclaimed Sassenachs. On the way back, a local farmer, also wearing a tam-o'-shanter and carrying a crook, looked on uneasily as a strange looking red-haired man wearing a bright burgundy cape led a small band of long-haired bohemians, including one disguised as a Scottish shepherd, back through the bracken. The shepherd's crook stayed with me, though I can't for the life of me remember how we managed to transport it home. Perhaps we all took turns holding it out of the car window.

Home for me and a now heavily pregnant Marge was provided by a French couple we'd befriended, who lived with their young son in a newly-built part of Hoddesdon. We hadn't lived there long when Marge's contractions became more intense and the ambulance was called. Soon after, on April the fourth, she gave birth to our son Micah, always known as Micky. In the waiting room of the Queen Alexandra hospital in Harlow, I couldn't understand why the other dads were pacing the floors and smoking as many cigarettes as the inhabitants of Whitley Bay. Then it struck me. They were all four,five, maybe ten years older, and unless you're particularly unfortunate, at nineteen you don't really worry about things like childbirth. Or much else, for that matter.

Life without industry is guilt, and industry without art is brutality
—John Ruskin.

Zoot would mimic my northern accent. I wasn't the slightest bit offended; in fact, I took it as a compliment. Who wants to be ignored? Anyway, he mimicked most people.

Beat Instrumental published a full page article on Zoot which started: "I've never wanted anything but a co-op group, but my name means more than it used to, so although it isn't a co-op in practice, we've got a co-op atmosphere". 'Let's shop at the Co-op!' (Alright, you need to be of a certain age to appreciate the connection to an early ad for the Co-operative stores). Further down the page: "Basically, though, I'm a solo artist; it's never been feasible for me to play with people I want to without being a solo artist'......'I'd like to develop away from a group'......'That's why with the new quartet I wanted to incorporate the new things that were happening, like lights and so on."

The man was mad! Mind you, he gave the three of us a name-check in my favourite magazine. I was dead chuffed—watch out *B.M.G.*, you're next.

Discounting the Alexis Korner radio show and the TV session in Stockholm, I hadn't worked in a studio since the recording of Tramline's *Moves of Vegetable Centuries* (that title!), so I was pleased when Zoot invited the three trusty lads to play on his forthcoming album. With a bit of luck he'd come up with a hit single and rid the top ten of novelty records like 'Two Little Boys' and 'Wanderin' Star', not to mention the mind-numbing 'Yellow River'. His manager had secured a deal with Polydor that nominated Alan Price as producer, and modern jazz musician/writer Keith Tippett as arranger for the brass and string parts. The studio was housed in an old converted church near Arsenal's football ground, yet far enough away from Finsbury Park to deter any psychosomatic reactions in my front teeth.

The musical and artistic direction was obvious from the first two tracks. In 'When Will You Know', we were given some insight into Zoot's way of thinking:

> "*Running and fighting for ever*
> *And writing my life into a script*
> *Trying to please the people I love*
> *So there will be no rift*"

Then, in 'When Tomorrow Comes':

"But when tomorrow comes
And I will see you cross the threshold
And your voice is not the echo of yesterday"

Mmm, well, it was 1970 after all. In 'Leaving It All Behind', Zoot balances precariously on the precipice of the deep and meaningful/meaningless:

"I have changed somehow
Things are different now in me
Now I think it's time to wake up
Before I know I'm gonna break up again
I'm gonna go and see if my mind will mend"

This particular track came complete with an underwater vocal effect that somehow found its way onto my scat-style guitar solo("…his jazz improvisations are first class"—Joe Bradley). However, the piece de resistance has got to be 'I Need Your Inspiration'.

What starts of as a mid-tempo gospel-tinged pop song is quickly dispelled by Barry Wilson's determination to enter the Guinness Book Of Records for the most drum fills in the shortest period of time. I follow closely in second place, soloing relentlessly with arguably the smallest guitar sound ever recorded, creating the impression that the instrument could be the size of a small oven glove. After three and a half minutes of laboured rhythms, the violin players launch into Keith Tippet's arrangement a la 'All You Need Is Love', spurred on no doubt by Zoot's continuous pleas for inspiration.

Suddenly, taking their cue from Mr Tippet, brass players begin soloing wildly with, and sometimes against, the oven glove guitar. As if this isn't enough, Zoot starts belting it out on piano. At this point the band breaks into a shuffle, and Alan Price is seen jumping around in the control room!

'Fuckin''ell man, ye canna whack it!' he may have said.

'Pardon?' the engineer may have responded.

Then, as if by magic, the tempo breaks again, and we're into the riff from the Beatles' 'Come Together'. I'd like to think that this was, once again, a pre-arrangement rather than an S.O.S. from some of the saner people in the room, but given the circumstances, I'm not so sure. To round it up, Zoot repeatedly suggests that we come together. Play together might have been a better recommendation.

As the song careers towards its frenzied climax, several of the older string players become disorientated, pack their instruments, and flee the building. One re-enters with an invoice. All that's missing is a liquid light show highlighting the title of Zoot's press release: All hope abandon, ye who enter the head of Money. Absolute madness!

A few days later Zoot showed us the proposed album cover. It was a painting of a medieval-period mother with a child sitting in her lap. The child's head had been replaced by a recent head shot of Zoot, gazing into the distance whilst the mother wept. Who could blame her? A face of innocence replaced by a cherubic-demonic face which fronted a head that contained a black festering secret. Interestingly, in the background a futuristic tower headed some kind of fiery jetty, whilst a couple of naked winged figures seemed to be attempting aerial sex. Other assorted objects included an orange, some sort of melted bauble, and a gorilla's shrunken head. Nothing unusual there, then. The right hand side of the painting continued on the back cover, and closer inspection revealed possible reasons why. Another naked winged figure half-knelt on the glans of a huge, limbed penis, with smoke billowing from it.

'Will you get away with that,' I asked innocently.

'Get away with what?' replied Zoot characteristically.

'You know, the thingie,' I ventured tactfully. He looked at me enquiringly.

'Ah, if they don't like the orange, bollocks to' em.'

Rock Star Status
The Final Chapter

Contrary to the romantic imagery presented by some rock journalists, the road does not go on forever. It merges into motorways, freeways and autobahns before offering you a huge choice of exits. Most performers choose to stop and re-fuel; some drive on into oblivion. However, the metaphorical journey does offer opportunity, which is something Leicester Forest East service station cannot boast in its CV.

Zoot and the band ran on for a little while longer, traversing that bygone university/college/club circuit which enabled professional musicians to work regularly and hone their craft. His eponymous solo album was released to, shall we say, tepid reviews, persuading him to halt proceedings and review his prospects. For me, the game was up; time to pull into that lay-by and await the old kismet. In the meantime, the French couple had decided to split up, presenting me, Marge and the baby with an accommodation problem. We took up temporary residence with another couple, in a council house in Harlow New Town, proving once and for all that I was definitely not in it for the glamour.

Juicy Lucy had appeared on the scene in 1969 and soon found themselves surrounded by controversy. Their debut album cover depicted a hugely overweight naked lady, Zelda Plum, languishing on a table amid a selection of squashed, sliced and strategically placed fruits. Probably shocking if you were over forty or hadn't seen the cover of Jimi Hendrix's *Electric Ladyland*, but my interests lay elsewhere (as Zelda obviously did). The band featured a true virtuoso, Glen 'Fernando' Campbell, whose name first came to my attention via the John Peel show a couple of years earlier, through his steel guitar playing with the Californian band, the Misunderstood. A band heavily influenced by the Yardbirds, they nevertheless created their own brand of exciting psychedelic blues, with Glenn very much to the fore. Juicy Lucy also featured saxophonist Chris Mercer, a refugee from John Mayall's big band with Mick Taylor.

Hang on, we've entered family tree territory here, so I'd better finish it off. Paul Williams had left Zoot Money's Big Roll Band and joined Mayall as bass player/occasional singer, playing alongside Mercer at some point. His down-home, bluesy vocals had obviously impressed the sax-man, as he was the natural choice to front Juicy Lucy when the original vocalist, Ray Owen, parted company with the band. Not long after, rhythm/lead guitarist Neil Hubbard left to help form the Grease Band with Henry McCullogh, thus offering an opportunity for a keen, young guitar player to impress. Thanks to Paul's recommendation, I got the gig. I met up with band at their get-away-from-it-all cottage near Peterborough to rehearse the set in readiness for my first gig.

Commuting to and from Harlow was inconvenient, and the over-all situation was not helped by the disappearance of some of Marge's clothes—the lady of the house's sister being the chief suspect. Once again, with Paul's help, we managed to secure a small, ill-equipped flat in Hammersmith. Judging by its initial appearance, it had only had one previous occupant—a goat. Still, with a bit of elbow-grease and other people's cast-offs, we managed to raise its appearance to that of a desir-able squat. If I'd been a comedian, it could have supplied me with enough material for a stage act:

'I wouldn't say our flat's damp, but the mice wear sou'westers'.

'It's not so much a toilet—more a latrine'.

'The wallpaper comes from a range called 'Inside the mind of Crippen''.

One of the neighbours had informed us that squatters had turned away in disgust, and that birds refused to fly over it, but I think he was winding us up. It might have been a dump, but at least it was our dump. Soon, I would celebrate my twentieth birthday, record my first album with Juicy Lucy, prepare for a tour of the United States, and never look back. For many years to come, I would be presented with undreamed of opportunities to indulge in most things known to man and beast.

But that's another story.

Index

saf publishing

info@safpublishing.com

www.safpublishing.com